# PLENTY - COUPS

# *PLENTY-COUPS*
## *Chief of the Crows*

FRANK B. LINDERMAN

*illustrated by*

H. M. Stoops

UNIVERSITY OF NEBRASKA PRESS • LINCOLN/LONDON

Originally published as *American: The Life Story of a Great Indian, Plenty-coups, Chief of the Crows*.



Bison Book Edition reprinted by arrangement with The John Day Company, Inc.

International Standard Book Number 0–8032–5121–1
Library of Congress Catalog Card Number 30–11369

First Bison Book printing: April, 1962

Most recent printing shown by first digit below:
9 10

Manufactured in the United States of America

*To My Grandson*

JAMES BEALE WALLER

## FOREWORD

PLENTY-COUPS (Aleek-chea-ahoosh, meaning Many Achievements) had been Chief of the Crows (Absarokees) ever since I knew anything about them. He was probably the last legitimate chieftain who had seen much of the old life of the plains Indian, and I have written his story as he told it to me so that a genuine record of his life might be preserved.

I am convinced that no white man has ever thoroughly known the Indian, and such a work as this must suffer because of the widely different views of life held by the two races, red and white. I have studied the Indian for more than forty years, not coldly, but with sympathy; yet even now I do not feel that I know much about him. He has told me many times that I *do* know him—that I have "felt his heart," but whether this is so I am not certain. And yet a stranger, after spending a week's vacation in our national parks, alternately fishing and talking to an English-speaking tribesman, will go home and glibly write all there is to learn about the habits, beliefs, and traditions of the Indian tribes of the Northwest.

Napoleon said after reading *The Iliad:* "I am

specially struck by the rude manners of the heroes, as compared with their lofty thoughts." The Indian has startled us by the same contrast, and so confounds us in our final estimate of the race we have conquered—from whom we might have learned needed lessons, if we had tried.

Now is too late. The real Indians are gone, and in the writings which will come from their descendants, we shall find difficulty in deciding between truth and falsehood concerning a life the writers could not have known. The change from a normal to an uncertain and unnatural existence came so suddenly to the plains Indian that his customs and traditions could not flourish, and they all but perished with the buffalo in the early eighties. One is startled that so brief a time could wipe away traditions ages old, and after contemplation wonders how much truth we know of ancient peoples.

The Crows as a tribe have always been friendly to white men, there being but a single instance of their tribal hostility. This was their farcical attempt in 1834 to starve out the traders at a post of the American Fur Company on the upper Missouri River, because the Company had located it in the territory of their bitter enemies, the Blackfeet. They fired no hostile shot, however, and made no attack on the fort, except to surround it quietly and pitch their lodges, which ten days later were dispersed by a single cannon-ball landed in their midst.

The Crows appear to me to be different from their neighbors in many respects [for one thing, they would not trade their furs for whisky], and I believe that at some time they came out of the South. They were almost constantly at war (mostly defensive) with the Sioux, Cheyenne, Arapahoe, and Blackfeet. This alone proves they were good fighting men, since, outnumbered as they were by such enemies, they could not otherwise have escaped annihilation.

But as I have said, the white man found them friendly, and soon began to use them against the tribes who disputed his way across Montana and into the Black Hills of South Dakota. He even gave them arms and ammunition, and besought the Government of the United States to do likewise. Chief Plenty-coups had in his possession a letter written by former Governor Potts of Montana territory beseeching the Government of the United States to arm the Crows, and saying in effect that the Crows when under arms were worth more to white settlers in the Northwest than all the army posts ever established.

F. B. L.

# PLENTY - COUPS

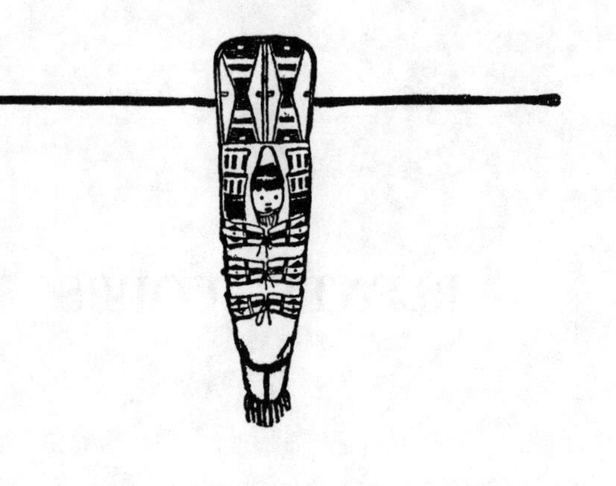

# I

PLENTY-COUPS, aided by Coyote-runs and Braided-scalp-lock, seated himself in the shade of the tall cottonwood trees that surround his cabin on Arrow Creek. "I am glad you have come, Sign-talker," he said, his nearly sightless eyes turned upon me. "Many men, both of my people and yours, have asked me to tell you the story of my life. This I have promised to do, and have sent for you; but why do you wish to write down my words, Sign-talker?"

The least suspicion that his story might count against him or his people would result in my failure to get a truthful tale of early Indian life on the plains. My answer must be honestly and carefully made.

"Because I do not believe there is any written story of an Indian chief's life," I said. "If you tell me what I wish to know, and I write it down, my people will better understand your people. The stories which I have written of Esacawata and the Crows have helped white children to know the children of your tribe. A better understanding between your people and mine will be good for both. Your story will help the men of my race to understand the men of your race."

Magpies jabbered above the racks of red meat hung to cure in the dry air, and the Chief's dogs, jealous and noisy, raced below them. By gift, the dogs would get very little of the meat they guarded; the magpies, more by theft.

"You are my friend, Sign-talker. I know your heart is good. I will tell you what you wish to know, and you may write it down," said Plenty-coups, at last. "I would have Coyote-runs and Plain-bull sit with us each day," he added. "I am an old man, and they will help me to remember."

"Good!" I agreed, glad of their company. They had known Plenty-coups all their lives and were different as two men could be. Plain-bull, thin and spare, was retiring; his badly scarred forehead was a reminder of strenuous life. Coyote-runs was tall and sturdy, his voice deep, and his manner aggressive. Both were old men, and both expressed satisfaction at the Chief's decision to tell me his story.

"If you do not tell all—if you forget—I will touch your moccasin with mine," Coyote-runs warned the old Chief, seriously. "We trust Sign-talker," he said. "Begin at the beginning. You are sunk in this ground here up to your armpits. You were told in your dream that you would have no children of your own blood, but that the Crows, all, would be your children. Your medicine-dream pointed the way of your life, and you have followed it. Begin at the beginning."

"He is more than eighty," I thought, when the Chief's face, upturned to the speaker, was in profile to me, its firm mouth and chin, its commanding nose and wide, fighting forehead, models for a heroic medallion. The broad-brimmed hat, with its fluttering eagle feather, hid the contour of his head. His gray hair fell in braids upon his broad shoulders. He had been a powerful man, not over-tall, and was now bent a little by the years. His deep chest and long arms told me that in his prime Plenty-coups had known few physical equals among his people. Could he, with one eye entirely gone and the other filmed by a cataract, distinguish Coyote-runs, I wondered.

He removed the hat from his head, laid it upon the grass beside him, and gripping the arms of the chair to steady himself, stood up. We all rose.

His fine head lifted, he turned as though his nearly sightless eyes could see the land he so much loves. "On this beautiful day, with its flowers, its sunshine, and green grass, a man in his right mind should speak straight to his friends. I will begin at the beginning," he said, and sat down again.

The company fell silent, as though waiting for me. Coyote-runs began filling his pipe, his eyes not watching his fingers. A score of questions came to my mind, but I banished them in the interest of order. "Where were you born?" I asked, while meadow larks trilled in the hay field.

"I was born eighty snows ago this summer [1848] at the place we call The-cliff-that-has-no-pass," said Plenty-coups slowly. "It is not far from the present site of Billings. My mother's name was Otter-woman. My father was Medicine-bird. I have forgotten the name of one of my grandmothers, but I remember her man's name, my grandfather's. It was Coyote-appears. My other grandmother, a Crow woman, married a man of the Shoshone. Her name was It-might-have-happened. She was my mother's mother."

Years ago I had heard that Plenty-coups was not a full-blooded Crow, but was part Shoshone. I knew that with the tribes of the Northwest a mother's blood determines both tribal and family relationship, but here was an opportunity for verification that ought to stand.

"With the blood of a Shoshone in your veins, do you consider yourself a full-blooded Crow?" I asked.

"Yes," he replied. "You are a white man and are thinking of my Shoshone grandfather, but remember that his woman, my grandmother, was a Crow and that all the women of my family were Crows."

"What are your earliest remembrances?" I asked, feeling that I had interrupted him with my question.

He smiled, his pipe ready to light. "Play," he said happily. "All boys are much alike. Their hearts are young, and they let them sing. We moved camp very often, and this to me, and the other boys of my age, was great fun. As soon as the crier rode through the village telling the people to get ready to travel, I would find my young friends and we would catch up our horses as fast as the herders brought them in. Lodges would come down quickly, horses would be packed, travois loaded, and then away we would go to some new place we boys had never seen before. The long line of pack-horses and travois reaching farther than we could see, the dogs and bands of loose horses, all sweeping across the rolling plains or up a mountain trail to some mysterious destination, made our hearts sing with joy.

"But even in all this we were not completely happy, because we were obliged to travel with the women and loaded travois. Young men, riding high-spirited horses whose hoofs scarcely touched the ground, would dash past us, and, showing off before the young women, race out of our sight. Then our mothers would talk among themselves, but so that we might hear.

" 'That young man on the white horse is Little-wolf, son of Medicine-woman,' one would say admiringly. 'He is brave, and so handsome.'

" 'Yes, and he has already counted coup and may marry when he chooses,' another would boast.

" 'Think of it!' another mother would exclaim. 'He has seen but twenty snows! Ah-mmmmm!' Perhaps she would lay her hand over her mouth, which is the sign for astonishment.

"This talking between our mothers, firing us with determination to distinguish ourselves, made us wish we were men. It was always going on—this talking among our elders, both men and women—and we were ever listening. On the march, in the village, everywhere, there was praise in our ears for skill and daring. Our mothers talked before us of the deeds of other women's sons, and warriors told stories of the bravery and fortitude of other warriors until a listening boy would gladly die to have his name spoken by the chiefs in council, or even by the women in their lodges.

"More and more we gathered by ourselves to talk and play. Often our talking was of warriors and war, and always in our playing there was the object of training ourselves to become warriors. We had our leaders just as our fathers had, and they became our chiefs in the same manner that men become chiefs, by distinguishing themselves."

The pleasure which thoughts of boyhood had brought to his face vanished now. His mind wandered from his story. "My people were wise," he said thoughtfully. "They never neglected the young or failed to keep before them deeds done by illustrious men of the tribe. Our teachers were willing and thorough. They were our grandfathers, fathers, or uncles. All were quick to praise excellence without speaking a word that might break the spirit of a boy who might be less capable than others. The boy who failed at any lesson got only more lessons, more care, until he was as far as he could go."

Age, to the Indian, is a warrant of experience and wisdom; white hair, a mark of the Almighty's distinction. Even scarred warriors will listen with deep respect to the counsel of elders, so that the Indian boy, schooled by example, readily accepts teaching from any elder. He is even flattered by the attention of grown men, and is therefore anxious to please.

"Your first lessons were with the bow and arrow?" I asked, to give him another start on his boyhood.

"Oh, no. Our first task was learning to run," he replied, his face lighting up again. "How well I remember my first lesson, and how proud I felt because my grandfather noticed me.

"The day was in summer, the world green and very beautiful. I was playing with some other boys when my grandfather stopped to watch. 'Take off your shirt and leggings,' he said to me.

"I tore them from my back and legs, and, naked except for my moccasins, stood before him.

" 'Now catch me that yellow butterfly,' he ordered. 'Be quick!'

"Away I went after the yellow butterfly. How fast these creatures are, and how cunning! In and out among the trees and bushes, across streams, over grassy places, now low near the ground, then just above my head, the dodging butterfly led me far before I caught and held it in my hand. Panting, but concealing my shortness of breath as best I could, I offered it to

Grandfather, who whispered, as though he told me a secret, 'Rub its wings over your heart, my son, and ask the butterflies to lend you their grace and swiftness.' "

The Indian of the Northwest (Montana and the surrounding country) believes that the Almighty gave each of His creations some peculiar grace or power, and that these favors, at least in part, may be obtained from them by him, if he is studious of their possessor's habits and emulates them to the limit of his ability. Here, I believe, is where the white man was first led to declare that the Indian believed in many gods. I have studied the Indian for more than forty years and have tried to understand him. He believes in one God, and has told me many times that he had never heard of the devil until "the Black-robes brought him" to his country. He does, however, believe there are created things which possess evil powers. Some of the tribes do not like the owl, believing him wicked. Others do not look upon him in this light, but respect him.

" 'O Butterflies, lend me your grace and swiftness!' I repeated, rubbing the broken wings over my pounding heart. If this would give me grace and speed I should catch many butterflies, I knew. But instead of keeping the secret I told my friends, as my grandfather knew I would," Plenty-coups chuckled, "and how many, many we boys caught after that to rub over our hearts. We chased butterflies to give us endurance in running, always rubbing our breasts with their wings, asking the butterflies to give us a portion of their power. We worked very hard at this, because running is necessary both in hunting and in war. I was never the swiftest among my friends, but not many could run farther than I."

"Is running a greater accomplishment than swimming?" I asked.

"Yes," he answered, "but swimming is more fun. In all seasons of the year most men were in the rivers before sunrise. Boys had plenty of teachers here. Sometimes they were hard on us, too. They would often send us into the water to swim among cakes of floating ice, and the ice taught us to take care of our bodies. Cold toughens a man. The buffalo-runners, in winter, rubbed their hands with sand and snow to prevent their fingers from stiffening in using the bow and arrow.

"Perhaps we would all be in our fathers' lodges by the fire when some teacher would call, 'Follow me, and do as I do!' Then we would run outside to follow him, racing behind him to the bank of a river. On the very edge he would turn a flip-flop into the water. Every boy who failed at the flip-flop was thrown in and ducked. The flip-flop was difficult for me. I was ducked many times before I learned it.

"We were eager to learn from both the men and the beasts who excelled in anything, and so never got through learning. But swimming was most fun, and therefore we worked harder at this than at other tasks. Whenever a boy's father caught a beaver, the boy got the tail and brought it to us. We would take turns slapping our joints and muscles with the flat beaver's tail until they burned under our blows. 'Teach us your power in the water, O Beaver!' we said, making our skins smart with the tail."

A woman wearing a pink calico dress and a red shawl came now to give the Chief a small bag full of something. I did not learn its contents. In her presentation the woman spoke rapidly and in a high-pitched voice, as though she were either excited or angry, and in his acceptance the Chief said not a word. He took the bag, laid it beside his hat on the grass, and the woman vanished. Nor was there any comment by either Coyote-runs or Plain-bull, and since the woman had used no signs with her rapid speech I could only hope that the visit had not seriously diverted the Chief from his story. But it had not. He began again, as though he had not broken off.

"I remember the day my father gave me a bow

and four arrows. The bow was light and small, the arrows blunt and short. But my pride in possessing them was great, since in spite of its smallness the bow was like my father's. It was made of cedar and was neatly backed with sinew to make it strong."

I knew he would take for granted that white men know how an Indian holds a bow and arrow, and I did not intend to permit this. There has been too much discussion over the proper position of the hands for me to let the opportunity to question him pass.

"Show me how you held your bow and arrow," I said.

He looked around his chair, as though searching for something he could not see. Coyote-runs guessed what was wanted, and, picking up a small cottonwood limb, quickly fashioned a rude bow. They both laughed merrily while Plain-bull found a smaller stick to serve as an arrow, and each in turn took a squint at its crookedness and shook his head. But it would do, and the Chief stood up with the improvised weapon. Gripping it firmly with his left hand, he deftly placed the arrow with his right, the index and second fingers straddling the shaft and, with the third finger, pulling the bow-string. The thumb's end was against the arrow notched into the string.

"Both hands and both arms must work together—at once," he said. "The left must push and the right must pull at the same time (so) if an arrow is to go straight or far. The left hand, grasping the bow, must be in its center. The right hand, palm toward one (like this), its fingers straddling the arrow (so), must know and keep the center of the bow-string without the eyes having to look."

The crooked arrow darted from the bow, swerved sharply, and struck the ground near a sleeping dog that bounded away as though chased. Coyote-runs and Plain-bull laughed. The Chief, sensing the cause, asked the reason, and then laughed with them.

"Nobody could tell where such an arrow would go," he said. "We always straightened our arrows with a bone straightener or with our teeth, before using them. First we shot for distance. No particular care was given to accuracy until the required distance was reached. Then we were taught to shoot with precision. This requires even more work than shooting for distance. My grandfather would place a buffalo-chip for me as a target. When I could put an arrow through its center three times out of five shots, he would roll the chip for me to shoot at. This was an exciting game, shooting at a rolling buffalo-chip. Sometimes our teachers would try a shot themselves.

"There never was any argument as to whose

arrow finally pinned the chip to the ground, because all arrow shafts were marked. Each boy knew his own arrows, and those of the other boys as well. Even the men of the tribe knew each other's arrows by their marks."

The marking of arrows was not only individual, but tribal. The Crows call the Cheyennes The-striped-feathered-arrows, because of the barred feathers of the wild turkey used on their arrow shafts. Even the sign-name for the Cheyennes was conceived from these feathers. It is made by drawing the right index finger several times across the left, as though making marks upon it.

"Speed in shooting was very necessary, since both in war and hunting a man must be quick to send a second arrow after his first. We were taught to hold one, and sometimes more arrows in the left hand with the bow. They were held points down, feathers up, so that when the right hand reached and drew them, the left would not be wounded by their sharp heads. Sometimes men carried an extra arrow in their mouths. This was quicker than pulling them from a quiver over the shoulder, but was a method used only in fighting, or dangerous situations."

He turned abruptly and spoke to Coyote-runs,

recalling an instance where an arrow held in the latter's mouth had saved his life. I was struck with the vividness of his motions, a thing that is utterly lost in description. An old Indian, interested in his tale, acts his part, and Plenty-coups' hands and body worked with his words as though the fight were *now*, and the speaking itself a war-song.

"The bow was the best of weapons for running the buffalo," he said, turning again to me. "Even the old-time white men, who had only the muzzle-loading guns, were quick to adopt the bow and arrow in running buffalo. But a powerful arm and a strong wrist are necessary to send an arrow deep into a buffalo. I have often seen them driven *through*."

The Indian buffalo-runner on his horse tried always to send his arrows forward and downward through the buffalo's paunch. If properly placed, they encountered no bones and were often driven down to the feathers—sometimes clear through. The paunch shot does not at once stop a buffalo, but it is nevertheless a mortal wound. It will soon cause the animal to drop out of the herd, sicken and die.

The early white trappers and hunters who came to the plains adopted the bow and arrow when running buffalo, because recharging their muzzle-loading guns was next to impossible on a running horse, especially on windy days.

"How old were you when you were given a genuine bow?" I asked.

"Seven," he answered. "When I was seven, my arrows had good iron points which my father got from the white trader on Elk River. This trader's name was Lumpy-neck."

The Crows call the Yellowstone "Elk River." The trader mentioned by Plenty-coups may have been Charles Larpenteur, who, I have been informed by a man who knew him, was afflicted with a goiter. Larpenteur traded along the Yellowstone down to the late 'sixties.

"But your bow was not very strong when you were seven years old," I said.

"No, of course not," he laughed. "But I thought it was strong. It was much stronger than my first one, and we hunted deer in the river bottoms and antelope on the plains. But our teachers were still our masters, and each day we had work to do.

"Sometimes when the camp was filled with drying meat, an uncle of some boy, or perhaps a grandfather, would walk through the village telling us secretly to meet at some place on the river bank. The place he selected would be timbered and shady, and there would be mud near at hand. As soon as we got the message, we would slip into our fathers' lodges and steal out a wolf's skin. Then we would run to the appointed place to meet our teacher. We knew what was intended, but each time the adventure was new to us, and we were like shadows slipping away from the village to the camp on the river bank.

"Our teacher had been a boy himself and knew just how we felt. When we were all met we seated ourselves to listen to what he had to tell us, and nobody who has not been a boy can know the thrills we had when our teacher stood up to speak to us as warriors. He did not mention *meat*. He called it *horses* and spoke in this fashion: 'Young men, there is an enemy village near us. Our Wolves [scouts] have seen it and counted many fine horses tied near the lodges. To enter this village and cut a fine horse is to count coup. See! I have here some nice coup-sticks.' He would hold up several peeled sticks to which were tied small breath-feathers of a war-eagle."

Entering an enemy's village and cutting the rope of a tied horse was called "cutting a horse." This deed entitled the performer to count "coup," while stealing a horse, or even a band of horses, on the open plains gave him no such honor. The downy feathers of the eagle, or of any other bird, are called "breath-feathers."

"Off would go our shirts and leggings. There was no talking, no laughing, but only carefully suppressed excitement while our teacher painted our bodies with the mud that was sure to be there. He made ears of it and set them on our heads, so that they were like the ears of wolves. When the mud dried a little, it became gray-looking and closely resembled a wolf's color. Down on our hands and knees, our teacher would cover our backs with the wolf skins we had stolen out of our fathers' lodges. Ho! Now we were a real party of Crow Wolves and anxious to be off."

For the moment Plenty-coups was a boy again. He spoke rapidly, his hands so swiftly telling the story in signs that I could catch only a part.

"We scattered then, each boy feeling the thrill a grown warrior knows when he is going into battle. I have felt them both, and they are the same. I shall never forget the first time I went in to steal meat.

" 'Now,' our teacher said when we were all ready, 'be Wolves! Go carefully. Beware of the old women. Bring back some good horses, and I will give you a feast.'

"The village was on Elk River, and the summer was old. The racks of drying meat stretched through the village, and in a little time I was near them, looking for a fine fat piece to carry away. But always a little farther along I thought I saw a fatter piece and, acting like a wolf, crept toward it, only to discover it was no better than the others. At last I said to myself, 'This will not do. Somebody will be seen. I will take this piece and go.'

"I raised myself up, my wolf skin dangling from my shoulders. Just as I took hold of the meat an old woman came out of a lodge on the other side of the rack. I stood very still, the wolf skin tickling my bare legs. I do not believe the old woman saw me, but somehow she had been made suspicious that everything was not right and kept looking around, as though she smelled something on the wind. She picked up a stick of wood and turned to go in again, her head still going from one side to the other. I thought she would go inside, but she didn't.

" 'Ho! Ho!' she cried out, dropping her stick of wood. 'The Magpies, the Magpies! Look out for your meat!'

"I was sure she had not seen me, but I must not stand there. I dropped quietly to my hands and knees and started away without any meat. Women were running from their lodges and calling out to one another, as though they expected to be killed, before I could reach the thick brush.

And that old woman caught me by the arm.

" 'Who are you?' she asked, looking sharply into my mud-covered face with eyes like knives.

"I didn't answer, even when she pinched my arm and shook me till my ribs rattled.

" 'Ha-ha-ha!' she laughed, dragging me to the river. 'I'll find out soon enough; I'll know you when I get this mud off.' She was a strong old woman and held me easily while she washed my face.

" 'Oh, it's you, is it?' she grunted, when my features showed through the mud. 'I thought I recognized you. Ha! I'll *give* you some meat, a good piece, too!' And she did. I had the best piece in the whole lot when I got back; but I could not say I stole it, because my face was clean."

Among the tribes of the plains a scout is called a "wolf," and scouts are made up as described. Wolves were everywhere, and therefore likely to be unnoticed. The sign for "scout" and "wolf" are nearly the same, while the sign for "smart man" differs only a little, the sign for "man" being added.

The uninformed have marked the Indian a stoic, and they have been wrong. The Indian is a natural man and loves a joke. He will laugh as readily as his white brother if he is among friends.

The chuckling of Plenty-coups while he was telling of the old woman who washed his face was immoderate and contagious. One day I sent him word that unless our interpreter kept his promise and sent me needed information, I might die of old age before this work was finished. He replied by messenger, "I know just how you feel. I myself am dying of old age waiting for the fulfillment of a promise made by the Government when I was an infant. They, at Washington, believe that I am still an infant, but who ever heard of an infant dying of old age?"

The three old men were now laughing merrily, each with some revived memory of a meat-stealing expedition. "Those were good days," said Plenty-coups, returning to his story.

"When the last boy was safely back at our meeting place, our teacher would go carefully over the pile of stolen meat, looking at each piece separately, as though examining a horse! 'This is a fine band of horses, a very, very fine band indeed. Ho! this is an especially fine horse! Who stole this one?' He would hold up a piece of back-fat.

" 'I did,' some boy would answer.

" 'Good! Here is a stick. Count coup, Fire-bull, Yellow-wing, or whoever it might be.'

"The lucky one would take the stick and poke

it into the ground before him. 'I stole this fine horse,' he would say, while we cheered him as though he had actually cut a horse in an enemy's village. But our teacher was always stingy with his offers of sticks, and sometimes only the best piece was counted.

"Then we feasted on the stolen meat, each boy telling at length what had happened to him in the village and just how he had acted. Those feasts were the sweetest I ever tasted. The stolen meat, roasted by our teacher, was the fattest and best-cooked of any I have known. But we worked very hard. Boys do not work today as we did. They do not appear to care if their bodies are strong."

Plenty-coups stopped talking and, with solemn face, refilled his pipe. His mood reached the others, even me. I could understand the grip of the old life better than one who has known nothing about it, and I wondered whether, in their sudden mood, they too heard the clatter of the white man's mowing machine in the hay field beyond the fence, and if it was not a noisy reminder of a malediction.

"We worked very hard," the Chief said again. "We never knew when we might be called by our teachers. Perhaps the morning would be cold and stormy, and we would all be sitting by our fathers' fires when some teacher would cry, 'All

Magpies come out!' And out we would come to follow wherever he led. He might lead us to the river, where ice-cakes floated thickly. And he might toss a handful of peeled sticks into the water, calling out, 'Go get them, Magpies!'

"While we stripped off our shirts and leggings, he would tell us that the boy who brought him the most sticks from the water might count coup. There was no waiting, no shirking. In we plunged amid the floating ice. The more difficulties we faced, the better for us, since they forced us to use our heads as well as our muscles. Nothing was overlooked that might lead us to self-reliance or give us courage in the face of sudden danger."

Magpies followed the Indian and were troublesome thieves where meat was curing on racks about his lodges. The term "magpies" when applied to the boys was equivalent to calling them "mischievous, persistent ones."

"One morning after I was eight years old we were called together by my grandfather. He had killed a grizzly bear the day before, and when we gathered near him I saw that he held the grizzly's heart in his hand. We all knew well what was expected of us, since every Crow warrior has eaten some of the heart of a grizzly bear, so that he may truthfully say, 'I have the heart of a grizzly!' I say this, even to this day, when there is trouble to face, and the words help me to keep my head. They clear my mind, make me suddenly calm."

Most tribes of the plains practice this custom. The grizzly bear is "always in his right mind," cool-headed, and ready for instant combat against any odds, even when roused from sleep. Therefore, to eat of the raw heart of the grizzly bear is to obtain self-mastery, the greatest of human attributes. I knew an old warrior who told me that he had once eaten a small portion of a human heart, the heart of an especially brave enemy, and that he had seen this done more than once when he was a young man. He was not a Crow, however.

"I felt myself growing stronger, more self-reliant, and cool from the day I ate a piece of that bear's heart. I believed I might soon be taken on war-parties, and with my friends began to play war."

Plenty-coups' thoughts now turned to those very days when mimic battles were fought with snowballs in winter, mud in summer. Soon the other old men were laughing with him over night attacks, victory, or rout. The mention of names, places, or valorous deeds animated their wrinkled faces. The party was merry, and I watched, as best I could, every sign that might let me know their fun. These sham battles usually followed the departure of a war-party for the enemy's country and were fought between two parties of boys under chosen leaders. I enjoyed their diversion, which I felt was refreshing the old man's mind, and had no thought of interrupting. But suddenly, as though he felt he had been impolite to me, the Chief stopped. "Forgive me," he smiled. "I am an old man and laugh very little." Then he took up his story exactly where he had left it.

"I hoped to become a chief, even then, and in my actions while playing games never permitted myself to be unjust to my companions. I tried hard to excel them in everything, and yet was very careful to let them see that I was fair. I soon became a leader among them, and they spoke my name with respect.

"My grandfather, who had given me my name, had told my mother that I should live to count many coups and be old. His dream had also told him that I should be a chief. 'I name him Aleek-chea-ahoosh [Many Achievements],' he told my mother, 'because in my dream I saw him count many coups.' Of course all the people knew this, and even as a boy I felt obliged to excel my companions, to be a leader among those of my own age. I must live up to my name, you see; and now I was beginning to think of dreaming."

The Indians of the Northwest are great believers in dreams. They starve and torture themselves in preparation for "medicine-dreams" and then repair alone to some difficult spot, generally a high mountain peak. There, without food or water, they spend four days and nights—if necessary, appealing to "helpers." Their condition, both physical and mental, is unbalanced by weakness brought on by abstaining from food, taking enervating sweat-baths, and continually courting fatigue. Their resulting dreams are weird and often terrifying, though sometimes wonderfully prophetic of the future. In a medicine-dream some animal, or bird, or "person" appears and offers "help." Sometimes these apparitions only give advice or teach the dreamer by parables which are later interpreted by the "wise ones" (medicine-men) of the tribe. Thereafter, or until he has had a greater dream (which seldom happens), the creature that offered help in his dream is the dreamer's medicine.

But "medicine" is a confusing term. It is not especially a curative. It is more nearly a protective property. It is a talisman or charm, a lucky piece that no old Indian will forego. It is always kept near him. Often, in formal camps, it is hung on a tripod back of his lodge if the lodge faces east.

"One day when the chokecherries were black and the plums red on the trees, my grandfather rode through the village, calling twenty of us older boys by name. The buffalo-runners had been out since daybreak, and we guessed what was before us. 'Get on your horses and follow me,' said my grandfather, riding out on the plains.

"We rode fast. Nothing was in sight until Grandfather led us over a hill. There we saw a circle of horsemen about one hundred yards across, and in its center a huge buffalo bull. We knew he had been wounded and tormented until he was very dangerous, and when we saw him there defying the men on horseback we began to dread the ordeal that was at hand.

"The circle parted as we rode through it, and the bull, angered by the stir we made, charged and sent us flying. The men were laughing at us when we returned, and this made me feel very small. They had again surrounded the bull, and I now saw an arrow sticking deep in his side. Only its feathers were sticking out of a wound that dripped blood on the ground.

" 'Get down from your horses, young men,' said my grandfather. 'A cool head, with quick feet, may strike this bull on the root of his tail with a bow. Be lively, and take care of yourselves. The young man who strikes, and is himself not hurt, may count coup.'

"I was first off my horse. Watching the bull, I slipped out of shirt and leggings, letting them fall where I stood. Naked, with only my bow in my right hand, I stepped away from my clothes, feeling that I might never see them again. I was not quite nine years old.

"The bull saw me, a human being afoot! He seemed to know that now he might kill, and he began to paw the ground and bellow as I walked carefully toward him.

"Suddenly he stopped pawing, and his voice was still. He came to meet me, his eyes green with anger and pain. I saw blood dropping from his side, not red blood now, but mixed with yellow.

"I stopped walking and stood still. This seemed to puzzle the bull, and he too stopped in his tracks. We looked at each other, the sun hot on my naked back. Heat from the plains danced on the bull's horns and head; his sides were panting, and his mouth was bloody.

"I knew that the men were watching me. I could feel their eyes on my back. I must go on. One step, two steps. The grass was soft and thick under my feet. Three steps. 'I am a Crow. I have the heart of a grizzly bear,' I said to myself. Three more steps. And then he charged!

"A cheer went up out of a cloud of dust. I had struck the bull on the root of his tail! But I was in even greater danger than before.

"Two other boys were after the bull now, but in spite of them he turned and came at me. To run was foolish. I stood still, waiting. The bull stopped very near me and bellowed, blowing bloody froth from his nose. The other boys, seeing my danger, did not move. The bull was not more than four bows' lengths from me, and I could feel my heart beating like a war-drum.

"Two large gray wolves crossed the circle just behind him, but the bull did not notice them, did not move an eye. He saw only me, and I was growing tired from the strain of watching him. I must get relief, must tempt him to come on. I stepped to my right. Instantly he charged—but I had dodged back to my left, across his way, and I struck him when he passed. This time I ran among the horsemen, with a lump of bloody froth on my breast. I had had enough."

At this ending Coyote-runs spoke up. "I saw him do that," he said proudly. "I was younger than he, but I was there and saw Plenty-coups strike the bull twice. No other boy struck him at all."

A fine-looking little boy, as full of life as a chipmunk but with only one good arm, came to the Chief's side. "The meat is cooked," he said, and ran away to Plenty-coups' house.

The old man turned to me. "You saw that little fellow has but one good arm, Sign-talker?" he asked very seriously.

"Yes," I answered.

"He was born like that. Times have changed. I never saw such a thing when I was a boy. I will tell you, later on, why such things come to people today. Will you eat with me?"

But I had brought my own lunch, and I ate it under the trees. There, beyond the end of the house, I could see the medicine-bundle of the Chief hung from a cottonwood limb. Wandering down to the historic spring, I drank and then sat watching the water bubble from beneath a rock to form the pool, which is housed and roofed. Mourning-doves cooed in the trees. Beyond Arrow Creek, by the Mission house, the war-drum of Bear-below was beating monotonously, and over in the hay field that belonged to Plenty-coups a white man was mowing grass with that clattering modern mower. Yesterday I had seen an airplane flying over the Chief's house. The past seemed desperately to clash with the present on the Crow reservation.

In an hour I went back to the house, and the Chief was ready to take up his story.

## II

"WHEN I was nine years old, a happening made me feel that I was a grown-up man, almost in a day," he said. "I had a brother. I shall not speak his name, but if there were four brave, handsome young men in our tribe my brother was one of them. I loved him dearly, and he was always an inspiration to me."

The names of the dead are seldom spoken by the Crows. "They have gone to their Father, Ah-badt-dadt-deah, and like Him are sacred." This custom makes the gathering of tribal history extremely difficult.

For a time Plenty-coups would not violate this

tribal custom which was threatening my success in getting his story. But finally, as his interest in his tale grew, he realized it was necessary, and graciously, and I believe a little fearfully, he named many men and women who had passed away.

"One morning when our village was going to move, he went on the war-trail against our enemy, the Lacota [Sioux]. All that day he was in my thoughts. Even when we crossed Elk River, where usually there was satisfying excitement, I kept thinking of my brother. Rafts had to be made for the old people and children, and these, drawn by four men on good horses, had ever given me plenty to think about. But this day nothing interested me. That night I could not sleep, even when all but the wolves were sleeping. When the village was set up on the Big River [Missouri], news reached us that my brother was gone—killed by Sioux on Powder River.

"My heart fell to the ground and stayed there. I mourned with my father and mother, and alone. I cut my flesh and bled myself weak. I knew now that I must dream if I hoped to avenge my brother, and I at once began to fast in preparation, first taking a sweat-bath to cleanse my body.

"Nobody saw me leave the village. I slipped away and climbed The-buffalo's-heart, where I fasted two more days and nights, without success. I saw nothing at all and gave up to travel back to my father's lodge, where I rested.

"The fourth night, while I was asleep, a voice said to me, 'You did not go to the right mountain, Plenty-coups.' I knew then that I should sometime succeed in dreaming.

"The village was preparing to move to the Little Rockies, a good place for me, and before the women began to take down the lodges I started out alone. Besides extra moccasins, I had a good buffalo robe, and as soon as I reached the mountains I covered a sweat-lodge with the robe and again cleansed my body. I was near the Two Buttes and chose the south one, which I climbed, and there I made a bed of sweet-sage and ground-cedar. I was determined that no smell of man should be on me and burned some *e-say* [a root that grows in the mountains] and sweet-sage, standing in their smoke and rubbing my body with the sage.

"The day was hot; and naked I began walking about the top of the mountain crying for Helpers, but got no answer, no offer of assistance. I grew more tired as the sun began to go toward the west, and finally I went to my bed, lying down so my feet would face the rising sun when he came again. Weakened by my walking and the days of fasting, I slept, remembering only the last rays of the sun as he went to his lodge. When I wakened, looking into the sky, I saw that The-seven-stars [the Big Dipper] had turned round The-star-that-does-not-move [North Star]. The night was westward. Morning was not far away, and wolves were howling on the plains far below me. I wondered if the village would reach the Little Rockies before night came again.

" 'Plenty-coups.'

"My name was spoken! The voice came from behind me, back of my head. My heart leaped like a deer struck by an arrow. 'Yes,' I answered, without moving.

" 'They want you, Plenty-coups. I have been sent to fetch you,' said the voice yet behind me, back of my head.

" 'I am ready,' I answered, and stood up, my head clear and light as air.

"The night had grown darker, and I felt rather than saw some Person go by me on my right side. I could not tell what Person it was, but thought he beckoned me.

" 'I am coming,' I said, but the Person made no answer and slipped away in a queer light that told me where he was. I followed over the same places I had traveled in the afternoon, not once feeling my feet touch a stone. They touched nothing at all where the way was rough, and without moccasins I walked in the Person's tracks as though the mountain were as smooth as the plains. My body was naked, and the winds cool and very pleasant, but I looked to see which way I was traveling. The stars told me that I was going east, and I could see that I was following the Person downhill. I could not actually see him, but I knew I was on his trail by the queer light ahead. His feet stirred no stone, nothing on the way, made no sound of walking, nor did mine.

"A coyote yelped on my right, and then another answered on my left. A little farther on I heard many coyotes yelping in a circle around us, and as we traveled they moved their circle along with us, as though they were all going to the same place as we. When the coyotes ahead stopped on a flat and sat down to yelp together, the ones behind closed in to make their circle smaller, all yelping loudly, as though they wished to tell the Person something. I knew now that our destination was not far off.

"The Person stopped, and I saw a lodge by his side. It seemed to rise up out of the ground. I saw that he came to it at its back, that it faced east, and that the Person reached its door by going around it to the right. But I did not know him, even when he coughed to let someone inside the lodge know he was there. He spoke no word to me but lifted the lodge door and stepped inside. 'Come, Plenty-coups, he said gently. And I too stepped into the lodge.

"There was no fire burning, and yet there was light in the lodge. I saw that it was filled with Persons I did not know. There were four rows of them in half-circles, two rows on each side of the center, and each Person was an old warrior. I could tell this by their faces and bearing. They had been counting coup. I knew this because before each, sticking in the ground, was a white coup-stick bearing the breath-feathers of a war-eagle. Some, however, used no stick at all, but only heavy first-feathers whose quills were strong enough to stick in the ground. These first-feathers were very fine, the handsomest I had ever seen, and I could not count them, they were so many.

" 'Why have you brought this young man into our lodge? We do not want him. He is not our kind and therefore has no place among us.' The words came from the south side, and my heart began to fall down.

"I looked to see what Persons sat on the south side, and my eyes made me afraid. They were the Winds, the Bad Storms, the Thunders, the Moon, and many Stars, all powerful, and each of them braver and much stronger than men."

I believe the Persons on the south side of the lodge, the Winds, Bad Storms, the Moon, and many Stars, were recognized by Plenty-coups as the great forces of nature, and that this is what he wished to convey to me.

" 'Come, Plenty-coups, and sit with *us.*' This voice was kind. It came from the north side.

" 'Sit,' said the Person who had brought me there, and then he was gone. I saw him no more.

"They, on the north side of the lodge, made a place for me. It was third from the head on the left, and I sat down there. The two parties of Persons were separated at the door, which faced the east, and again in the west, which was the head of the lodge, so that the Spirit-trail from east to west was open, if any wished to travel that way. On neither side were the Persons the same as I. All were different, but I knew now that they had rights in the world, as I had, that Ah-badt-dadt-deah had created them, as He had me and other men. Nobody there told me this, but I felt it in the lodge as I felt the presence of the Persons. I knew that to live on the world I must concede that those Persons across the lodge who had not wished me to sit with them had work to do, and that I could not prevent them from doing it. I felt a little afraid but was glad I was there.

" 'Take these, Plenty-coups.' The Person at

the head of the lodge on the north side handed me several beautiful first-feathers of a war-eagle.

"I looked into his eyes. He was a Dwarf-person, chief of the Little-people who live in the Medicine-rock, which you can almost see from here, and who made the stone arrow points. I now saw that all on my side were the same as he, that all were Dwarfs not tall as my knee."

The Dwarfs or Little-people are legendary beings, supposed to possess great physical strength. In the story of "Lost Boy," a Crow saw one of the Dwarfs shoulder a full-grown bull elk and walk with it on his shoulder. They dwell in Medicine-rock, near Pryor, Montana. The Little-people made the stone arrow heads, the Crows believe.

All the Indian tribes of the Northwestern plains, with whom I am acquainted, possess legends that deal with the makers of the stone arrow points which are scattered so plentifully over North America. These legends, together with the knowledge that identical stone arrow points are found in Europe, led me, long ago, to the belief that our plains Indians neither made nor used them—that some other people made them. Careful inquiry among very old Indians, beginning in 1886, has not discovered a single tribesman who had ever heard of his own people making stone arrow points. These old men have told me that before the white man came their arrow points were of bone.

" 'Stick one of your feathers in the ground before you and count coup,' said the Dwarf-chief.

"I hesitated. I had never yet counted coup, and here in this lodge with old warriors was no place to lie.

" 'Count coup!' commanded the Dwarf-chief.

"I stuck a first-feather into the ground before me, fearing a dispute.

" 'That,' said the Dwarf-chief, 'is the rider of the *white* horse! I first struck him with my coup-stick, and then, while he was unharmed and fighting, I took his bow from him.'

"The Thunders, who sat at the head of the lodge on the south side, said, 'Nothing can be better than that.'

" 'Stick another feather before you, Plenty-coups,' said the Dwarf-chief.

"I stuck another first-feather in the ground, wondering what the Dwarf-chief would say for it. But this time I was not afraid.

" 'That,' he said, 'is the rider of the *black* horse. I first struck him with my bow. Then, while he was armed with a knife and fighting me, I took his bow from him, also his shield.'

"'Enough!' said the Persons on the south side. 'No Person can do better than that.'

"'Let us leave off counting coups. We are glad you have admitted this young man to our lodge,' said the Bad Storms, 'and we think you should give him something to take back with him, some strong medicine that will help him.'

Plenty-coups had been speaking rapidly, his hands following his spoken words with signs, acting parts, while his facial expressions gave tremendous emphasis to his story. He was perspiring and stopped to brush his face with his hand.

"I had not spoken," he went on, "and could not understand why the Dwarf-chief had ordered me to stick the feathers, nor why he had counted coups in my name before such powerful Persons.

"'He will be a Chief,' said the Dwarf-chief. 'I can give him nothing. He already possesses the power to become great if he will use it. Let him cultivate his senses, let him use the powers which Ah-badt-dadt-deah has given him, and he will go far. The difference between men grows out of the use, or non-use, of what was given them by Ah-badt-dadt-deah in the first place.'

"Then he said to me, 'Plenty-coups, we, the Dwarfs, the Little-people, have adopted you and will be your Helpers throughout your life on this world. We have no medicine-bundle to give you. They are cumbersome things at best and are often in a warrior's way. Instead, we will offer you advice. Listen!

" 'In you, as in all men, are natural powers. You have a will. Learn to use it. Make it work for you. Sharpen your senses as you sharpen your knife. Remember the wolf smells better than you do because he has learned to depend on his nose. It tells him every secret the winds carry because he uses it all the time, makes it work for him. We can give you nothing. You already possess everything necessary to become great. Use your powers. Make them work for you, and you will become a Chief.' "

A medicine-bundle contains the medicine or talisman of its possessor. Often the skin and stuffed head of an animal as large as a wolf is used. Sometimes, however, the bundles are small, containing the skin, claws, teeth, or heads of lesser creatures, depending wholly upon what animal or bird offered "help" to the dreamer. The medicine-bundle is of first importance, the possessor believing implicitly that the superlative power of the animal or bird that offered aid in his dream is always at hand and at his service when he is in need. The contents of these bundles are secret and sacred to the Indian.

"When I wakened, I was perspiring. Looking

into the early morning sky that was growing light in the north, I went over it all in my mind. I saw and understood that whatever I accomplished must be by my own efforts, that I must myself do the things I wished to do. And I knew I could accomplish them if I used the powers that Ah-badt-dadt-deah had given me. I *had* a will and I would use it, make it work for me, as the Dwarf-chief had advised. I became very happy, lying there looking up into the sky. My heart began to sing like a bird, and I went back to the village, needing no man to tell me the meaning of my dream. I took a sweat-bath and rested in my father's lodge. I *knew* myself now."

## III

HERE the old Chief, as though struck with remorse, turned his head aside and whispered, "O Little-people, you who have been my good Helpers through a long life, forgive me if I have done wrong in telling this to Sign-talker. I believed I was doing right. Be kind. I shall see you very soon and explain all."

He appeared shaken, and I wondered if he would go on. Coyote-runs and Plain-bull felt as much relieved as I did when the old man said, "I was nine years old and undeveloped, but I realized the constant danger my people were in from enemies on every side. Our country is the most beautiful of all. Its rivers and plains, its mountains and timber lands, where there was always plenty of meat and berries, attracted other tribes, and they wished to possess it for their own.

"To keep peace our chiefs sent out clans to the north, east, south, and west. They were to tell any who wished to come into our country that they were welcome. They were told to say, 'You may hunt and may gather berries and plums in our country, but when you have all you can carry you must go back to your own lands. If you do this all will be well. But if you remain overlong, we will warn you to depart. If you are foolish and do not listen, your horses will be stolen; and if even this does not start you homeward, we will attack you and drive you out.' "

The country belonging to the Crows was not only beautiful, but it was the very heart of the buffalo range of the Northwest. It embraced endless plains, high mountains, and great rivers, fed by streams clear as crystal. No other section could compare with the Crow country, especially when it was untouched by white men. Its wealth in all kinds of game, grass, roots, and berries made enemies for the Crows, who, often outnumbered, were obliged continually to defend it against surrounding tribes.

"These clans did not go to the other people, but camped near the boundaries of our domain so that they might speak to any visitor coming from any direction and give him the message from our chiefs. But little heed was paid to what we said. There was almost continual war with those who coveted our country.

"The Lacota [Sioux], Striped-feathered-arrows [Cheyennes], and Tattooed-breasts [Arapahoes] kept pushing us back, away from the Black Hills, until finally when I was a young man we were mostly in the country of the Bighorn and Little Bighorn rivers. These tribes, like the Pecunies [Piegans], Bloods, and Blackfeet [all Blackfeet], had many guns which they had obtained from white traders, while we had almost no guns in the tribe. The northern tribes could easily trade with the Hudson's Bay people, while the tribes eastward of us traded furs and robes to the American Fur Company for guns, powder, and lead.

"There is no better weapon than the bow for running buffalo, but in war the gun is often the best. All tribes were against us, the Blackfeet north and west, the Cheyennes and Sioux east, the Shoshones and Arapahoes on the south; and besides these there was often war with the Flatheads, Assiniboines, and Hairy-noses [Gros Ventres of the prairies]."

Plenty-coups stopped to light his pipe. "Which of all the tribesmen your people have met in war are the bravest?" I asked.

He did not hesitate an instant. "The Striped-feathered-arrows [Cheyennes]," he said. "And next are the Flatheads. A Flathead will not run. He will drop his robe [die where he stands]."

"How about the Pecunies [Piegans]?" I asked, struck by his earnestness.

He thought a minute. "If a Pecunie's belly is full, he is sure to go to sleep," he chuckled.

"The Absarokees [Crows] are a different people from any of these," he went on. "We have no relatives except the Dirt-lodges, called by the white men, 'Gros Ventres.' We were obliged to fight alone, and we *could* fight. Our chiefs were able men when I was a boy. They were Long-horse, Sits-in-the-middle-of-the-land, Thin-belly, and Iron-bull. How they inspired me, a boy, aching for age and opportunity!

"We followed the buffalo herds over our beautiful plains, fighting a battle one day and sending out a war-party against the enemy the next. My heart was afire. I wished so to help my people, to distinguish myself, so that I might wear an eagle's feather in my hair. How I worked to make my arms strong as a grizzly's, and how much I practiced with my bow! A boy never wished to be a man more than I."

The Earth-lodges, or Dirt-lodges, often con-founded by white men with the Gros Ventres, or

Hairy-noses, are related to the Crows. Both tribes tell the same story of their separation, which occurred long in the past and was the result of a quarrel between two women over the possession of a buffalo's paunch. After the disagreement the Crows (Absarokees) moved to the "Long Mountain," the "Story-land," where they have since remained. Before the separation the combined tribes built earth-lodges, established fairly permanent villages, and cultivated fields of corn and pumpkins; but after the division the Crows became more nomadic than formerly and, like the other tribes of the plains, followed the buffalo herds.

There are two tribes that, with the white man, bear the name of "Gros Ventres," but the rightful owners of the name are the Gros Ventres of the prairies, an offshoot of the Arapahoes, according to the Crows, who call them the Hairy-noses.

The sign-name for the Earth-lodges is made by the motions of shelling an ear of corn, while the sign-name for the Crows is made by imitating with the hands the moving wings of a bird. But Absarokee does not mean Crow. The name seems to have been given them by the early French voyageurs, who may have got it from the Sioux. "Absanokee," as the word was originally pronounced, means more nearly "descendants of the Raven," or "children of the Raven." Besides, the tribe's "medicine," or protecting jinn, is the raven.

"One windy day," the Chief went on, "when the clouds touched their peaks, we came to the Beartooth Mountains. I saw many lodges among the trees there and thought at first they belonged to our enemies, the Blackfeet. But they were Crow lodges, and all the clans, even those that had been farthest away, had come to the mountains to meet the chiefs in council. I was glad to see them all. I was born a Burned-mouth, but had been raised by the Newly-made-lodges. Both were here, with the Whistling-waters, the Big-lodges, the Kicked-in-the-bellies, and the others. The sight of so large a village under the pine trees, the air-clear water racing past it to the plains, the smell of smoke from lodge-fires, the sound of war-drums and happy voices, made my heart sing.

"That day I walked with my first sweetheart. I will not speak her name. She went away to her Father before we could marry, but I know, even to this day, where they buried her. I have never forgotten."

I learned later that this young woman's name was Two-buffaloes.

"That night the secret societies held meetings,

the Foxes, the War-clubs, the Big-dogs, the Crazy-dogs, the Muddy-hands, the Fighting-bulls, and others. Bright fires blazed and crackled among the pines, and drums were going all night long. I wished with all my heart that I might belong to one of these secret societies. I thought most of the Foxes, and I looked with longing eyes at their firelit lodge, where men spoke of things I could not know. But I was yet only a boy."

These secret societies possessed great influence over their members, so much that I believe them in a measure responsible even today for the lack of unity that sometimes presents itself in the administration of tribal affairs. They were quite different from the clans. A man or woman was born to a clan, while the societies elected their members upon petition. Any warrior who had counted coup was eligible and might if accepted be initiated by ordeals into the society of his choice. However, in case of the death of a member, a blood brother of the deceased had the right to demand initiation and his place in the society. I know of but one society among the Crows whose membership was confined to a particular class. This was the Fighting-bulls, whose membership was made up of aged fighting men.

The policing of the villages was left to these

societies, especially to the War-clubs and the Foxes, and this duty required much vigilance. Young men, too, often went to war alone, and the police had difficulty in keeping them in camp. There was no stealing among the tribesmen. Only little children took things that did not belong to them, and these were returned without wrangling. The policing society saw to it that guards were posted, "that lovers behaved themselves," and that scouts did their duty. Asked if he had ever known of murder among his tribesmen, Plenty-coups replied, "No, but I have known of Crow warriors mistaking another Crow for an enemy and killing him. When this happened, the careless one was made to care for those who had depended upon the dead man for support. And this was all we did about it."

The Foxes and War-clubs were most respected, because of their traditions, which were ages old. Each possessed two coup-sticks, tribal in their significance and carried by individual members from the time of appointment until snow fell again upon their heads (supposed to be one year). One of these sticks in each society was straight and bore one eagle's feather on its smaller end. If in battle its carrier stuck this stick into the ground, he must not retreat or leave the stick. He must drop his robe [die] there unless relieved by a brother member of his society riding between him and the enemy. He might then move the stick with honor, but while it was sticking in the ground it represented the Crow country. The bearers of the crooked sticks, each having two feathers, might at their discretion move them to better stands after sticking them to mark a position. But they must die in losing them to the enemy. By striking coup with any of these society coup-sticks, the bearers counted double, two for one, since their lives were in greater danger while carrying them. They were self-appointed. The chiefs, after asking who would next carry the sticks, passed the pipe. If a man took it and smoked, he thus engaged to carry one of the sticks for a season. I asked Plenty-coups if he had ever carried a society coup-stick. He said that he had. "But I was lucky. Nothing happened when I carried the straight stick for the Foxes. I was just twenty-one," he said.

To count coup a warrior had to strike an armed and fighting enemy with his coup-stick, quirt, or bow before otherwise harming him, or take his weapons while he was yet alive, or strike the first enemy falling in battle, no matter who killed him, or strike the enemy's breastworks while under fire, or steal a horse tied to a lodge in an enemy's camp, etc. The first named was the most honorable, and to strike such a coup a warrior would often display great bravery. An eagle's feather worn in the hair was a mark of distinction and told the world that the wearer had counted coup. He might wear one for each coup he counted "if he was that kind of man," Plenty-coups said. But if a warrior was wounded in counting coup, the feather he wore to mark the event must be painted red to show that he bled. Strangely enough from our point of view, this was not considered so great an honor as escaping unharmed. After a battle, or exploit, by one or more individuals there ensued the ceremony of counting coup, relating adventures. This is the custom that led the white man to declare the Indian a born boaster. Some of the tribes of the Northwest added an eagle's feather to their individual coup-stick for each coup counted. But the Crows did not follow this custom.

"We feasted there," said Plenty-coups. "Fat meat of bighorn, deer, and elk was plentiful. The hunters had killed many of these animals because they knew there would soon be a very large village to feed. Besides, light skins were always needed for shirts and leggings. Even the dogs found more than they could eat near that village, and our horses, nearly always feasting on rich grass, enjoyed the change the mountains gave them. All night the drums were beating, and in the light of fires that smelled sweet the people danced until they were tired.

"I was wakened by a crier. He was riding through the village with some message from the council of the night before. I sat up to listen. 'There are high peaks in these mountains, O young men! Go to them and dream!' the crier said. 'Are you men, or women? Are you afraid of a little suffering? Go into these mountains and find Helpers for yourselves and your people who have so many enemies!'

"I sat there in my robe, listening till his voice was far off. How I wished to count coup, to wear an eagle's feather in my hair, to sit in the council with my chiefs, holding an eagle's wing in my hand."

To carry an eagle's wing at tribal ceremonies was a mark of distinction. Sometimes the quills of the feathers were beautifully covered with colored porcupine quills and the wing was used as a fan.

"I got up from my robe. The air was cool and smelled of the trees outside. Ought I to go again and try to dream?

" 'Go, young man!'

"Another crier had started through the village.

His first words answered my unspoken question. I walked out of the lodge, only half hearing the rest of his message. The sun was just coming, and the wind was in the treetops. Women were kindling their fires, and hunters were leaving the camp when I started out alone.

"I decided to go afoot to the Crazy Mountains, two long days' journey from the village. The traveling without food or drink was good for me, and as soon as I reached the Crazies I took a sweat-bath and climbed the highest peak. There is a lake at its base, and the winds are always stirring about it. But even though I fasted two more days and nights, walking over the mountain top, no Person came to me, nothing was offered. I saw several grizzly bears that were nearly white in the moonlight, and one of them came very near to me, but he did not speak. Even when I slept on that peak in the Crazies, no bird or animal or Person spoke a word to me, and I grew discouraged. I could not dream.

"Back in the village I told my closest friends about the high peaks I had seen, about the white grizzly bears, and the lake. They were interested and said they would go back with me and that we would all try to dream.

"There were three besides myself who set out, with extra moccasins and a robe to cover our sweat-lodge. We camped on good water just below the peak where I had tried to dream, quickly took our sweat-baths, and started up the mountains. It was already dark when we separated, but I found no difficulty in reaching my old bed on the tall peak that looked down on the little lake, or in making a new bed with ground-cedar and sweet-sage. Owls were hooting under the stars while I rubbed my body with the sweet-smelling herbs before starting out to walk myself weak.

"When I could scarcely stand, I made my way back to my bed and slept with my feet toward the east. But no Person came to me, nothing was offered; and when the day came I got up to walk again over the mountain top, calling for Helpers as I had done the night before.

"All day the sun was hot, and my tongue was swollen for want of water; but I saw nothing, heard nothing, even when night came again to cool the mountain. No sound had reached my ears, except my own voice and the howling of wolves down on the plains.

"I knew that our great Crow warriors of other days sacrificed their flesh and blood to dream, and just when the night was leaving to let the morning come I stopped at a fallen tree, and, laying the first finger of my left hand upon the log, I cut part of it off with my knife. [The end of the left index finger on the Chief's hand is missing].

But no blood came. The stump of my finger was white as the finger of a dead man, and to make it bleed I struck it against the log until blood flowed freely. Then I began to walk and call for Helpers, hoping that some Person would smell my blood and come to aid me.

"Near the middle of that day my head grew dizzy, and I sat down. I had eaten nothing, taken no water, for nearly four days and nights, and my mind must have left me while I sat there under the hot sun on the mountain top. It must have traveled far away, because the sun was nearly down when it returned and found me lying on my face. As soon as it came back to me I sat up and looked about, at first not knowing where I was. Four war-eagles were sitting in a row along a trail of my blood just above me. But they did not speak to me, offered nothing at all.

"I thought I would try to reach my bed, and when I stood up I saw my three friends. They had seen the eagles flying over my peak and had become frightened, believing me dead. They carried me to my bed and stayed long enough to smoke with me before going back to their own places. While we smoked, the four war-eagles did not fly away. They sat there by my blood on the rocks, even after the night came on and chilled everything living on the mountain."

Again the Chief whispered aside to the Little-people, asking them if he might go on. When he finally resumed, I felt that somehow he had been reassured. His voice was very low, yet strained, as though he were tiring.

"I dreamed. I heard a voice at midnight and saw a Person standing at my feet, in the east. He said, 'Plenty-coups, the Person down there wants you now.'

"He pointed, and from the peak in the Crazy Mountains I saw a Buffalo-bull standing *where we are sitting now*. I got up and started to go to the Bull, because I knew he was the Person who wanted me. The other Person was gone. Where he had stood when he spoke to me there was nothing at all.

"The way is very long from the Crazies to this place where we are sitting today, but I came here quickly in my dream. On that hill over yonder was where I stopped to look at the Bull. He had changed into a Man-person wearing a buffalo robe with the hair outside. Later I picked up the buffalo skull that you see over there, on the very spot where the Person had stood. I have kept that skull for more than seventy years.

"The Man-person beckoned me from the hill over yonder where I had stopped, and I walked to where he stood. When I reached his side he began to sink slowly into the ground, right over there [pointing]. Just as the Man-person was disappearing he spoke. 'Follow me,' he said.

"But I was afraid. 'Come,' he said from the darkness. And I got down into the hole in the ground to follow him, walking bent-over for ten steps. Then I stood straight and saw a small light far off. It was like a window in a white man's house of today, and I knew the hole was leading us toward the Arrow Creek Mountains [the Pryors].

"In the way of the light, between it and me, I could see countless buffalo, see their sharp horns thick as the grass grows. I could smell their bodies and hear them snorting, ahead and on both sides of me. Their eyes, without number, were like little fires in the darkness of the hole in the ground, and I felt afraid among so many big bulls. The Man-person must have known this, because he said, 'Be not afraid, Plenty-coups. It was these Persons who sent for you. They will not do you harm.'

"My body was naked. I feared walking among them in such a narrow place. The burrs that are always in their hair would scratch my skin, even if their hoofs and horns did not wound me more deeply. I did not like the way the Man-person went among them. 'Fear nothing! Follow me, Plenty-coups,' he said.

"I felt their warm bodies against my own, but went on after the Man-person, edging around them or going between them all that night and all the next day, with my eyes always looking ahead at the hole of light. But none harmed me, none even spoke to me, and at last we came out of the hole in the ground and saw the Square White Butte at the mouth of Arrow Creek Canyon. It was on our right. White men call it Castle Rock, but our name for it is The-fasting-place.

"Now, out in the light of the sun, I saw that the Man-person who had led me had a rattle in his hand. It was large and painted red. [The rattle is used in ceremonials. It is sometimes made of the bladder of an animal, dried, with small pebbles inside, so that when shaken it gives a rattling sound.] When he reached the top of a knoll he turned and said to me, 'Sit here!'

"Then he shook his red rattle and sang a queer song four times. 'Look!' he pointed.

"Out of the hole in the ground came the buffalo, bulls and cows and calves without number. They spread wide and blackened the plains. Everywhere I looked great herds of buffalo were going in every direction, and still others without number were pouring out of the hole in the ground to travel on the wide plains. When at last they ceased coming out of the hole in the ground, all were gone, *all!* There was not one in sight anywhere, even out on the plains. I saw a few antelope on a hillside, but no buffalo—not a bull, not a cow, not one calf, was anywhere on the plains.

"I turned to look at the Man-person beside me. He shook his red rattle again. 'Look!' he pointed.

"Out of the hole in the ground came bulls and cows and calves past counting. These, like the others, scattered and spread on the plains. But they stopped in small bands and began to eat the grass. Many lay down, not as a buffalo does but differently, and many were spotted. Hardly any two were alike in color or size. And the bulls bellowed differently too, not deep and far-sounding like the bulls of the buffalo but sharper and yet weaker in my ears. Their tails were different, longer, and nearly brushed the ground. They were not buffalo. These were strange animals from another world.

"I was frightened and turned to the Man-person, who only shook his red rattle but did not sing. He did not even tell me to look, but I did look and saw all the Spotted-buffalo go back into the hole in the ground, until there was nothing except a few antelope anywhere in sight.

" 'Do you understand this which I have shown you, Plenty-coups?' he asked me.

" 'No!' I answered. How could he expect me to understand such a thing when I was not yet ten years old?

"During all the time the Spotted-buffalo were

going back into the hole in the ground the Man-person had not once looked at me. He stood facing the south as though the Spotted-buffalo belonged there. 'Come, Plenty-coups,' he said finally, when the last had disappeared.

"I followed him back through the hole in the ground without seeing anything until we came out *right over there* [pointing] where we had first entered the hole in the ground. Then I saw the spring down by those trees, this very house just as it is, these trees which comfort us today, and a very old man sitting in the shade, alone. I felt pity for him because he was so old and feeble.

" 'Look well upon this old man,' said the Man-person. 'Do you know him, Plenty-coups?' he asked me.

" 'No,' I said, looking closely at the old man's face in the shade of *this* tree.

" 'This old man is yourself, Plenty-coups,' he told me. And then I could see the Man-person no more. He was gone, and so too was the old man.

"Instead I saw only a dark forest. A fierce storm was coming fast. The sky was black with streaks of mad color through it. I saw the Four Winds gathering to strike the forest, and held my breath. Pity was hot in my heart for the beautiful trees. I felt pity for all things that lived in that forest, but was powerless to stand with them against the Four Winds that together were making war. I shielded my own face with my arm when they charged! I heard the Thunders calling out in the storm, saw beautiful trees twist like blades of grass and fall in tangled piles where the forest had been. Bending low, I heard the Four Winds rush past me as though they were not yet satisfied, and then I looked at the destruction they had left behind them.

"Only one tree, tall and straight, was left standing where the great forest had stood. The Four Winds that always make war alone had this time struck together, riding down every tree in the forest but *one*. Standing there alone among its dead tribesmen, I thought it looked sad. 'What does this mean?' I whispered in my dream.

" 'Listen, Plenty-coups,' said a voice. 'In that tree is the lodge of the Chickadee. He is least in strength but strongest of mind among his kind. He is willing to work for wisdom. The Chickadee-person is a good listener. Nothing escapes his ears, which he has sharpened by constant use. Whenever others are talking together of their successes or failures, there you will find the Chickadee-person listening to their words. But in all his listening he tends to his own business. He never intrudes, never speaks in strange company, and yet never misses a chance to learn from others. He gains success and avoids failure by learning how others succeeded or failed, and without great trouble to himself. There is scarcely a lodge he does not visit, hardly a Person he does not know, and yet everybody likes him, because he minds his own business, or pretends to.

" 'The lodges of countless Bird-people were in that forest when the Four Winds charged it. Only one is left unharmed, the lodge of the Chickadee-person. Develop your body, but do not neglect your mind, Plenty-coups. It is the mind that leads a man to power, not strength of body.'

## IV

"I WAKENED then. My three friends were standing at my feet in the sunshine. They helped me stand. I was very weak, but my heart was singing, even as my friends half carried me to the foot of the mountain and kindled a fire. One killed a deer, and I ate a little of the meat. It is not well to eat heartily after so long a time of fasting. But the meat helped me to recover my strength a little. Of course we had all taken sweat-baths before touching the meat, or even killing the deer, and I was happy there beside the clear water with my friends. Toward night two of them went back to the village to bring horses for me and the man who stayed with me at the foot of the mountains. I was yet too weak to travel so far afoot.

"Lying by the side of the clear water, looking up into the blue sky, I kept thinking of my dream, but could understand little of it except that my medicine was the Chickadee. I should have a small medicine-bundle, indeed. And I would call upon the Wise Ones [medicine-men] of the tribe to interpret the rest. Perhaps they could tell the meaning of my dream from beginning to end.

"In the middle of the third day my ears told me that horses were coming. My friend and I walked a little way to meet them, and very soon I heard the voices of my uncles, White-horse and Cuts-the-turnip. They were singing the Crow Praise Song with several others who were leading extra horses for my friend and me.

"I was stronger now and could ride alone, but the way seemed very far indeed. Of course I had spoken to nobody of my dream, but when I came in sight of the village my uncles began again to sing the Praise Song, and many people came out to meet us. They were all very happy, because they knew I now had Helpers and would use my power to aid my people.

"None spoke to me, not because he did not

wish to be kind but because the people knew I must first cleanse myself in a sweat-lodge before going about the village with my friends. I saw my young sweetheart by her father's lodge, and although she did not speak to me I thought she looked happier than ever before.

"While I was in the sweat-lodge my uncles rode through the village telling the Wise Ones that I had come, that I had dreamed and wished interpretation of my vision in council. I heard them calling this message to those who had distinguished themselves by feats of daring or acts of wisdom, and I wondered what my dream could mean, what the Wise Ones would say to me after I had told them all I had seen and heard on the peak in the Crazy Mountains. I respected them so highly that rather than have them speak lightly of my dream I would willingly have died."

Plenty-coups hesitated, his dimmed eyes staring over my head into the past. His last words, spoken in a whisper, had lifted him away. He had forgotten me and even the two old men who, like himself, appeared to be under a spell and scarcely breathed.

"My father was gone," the Chief went on, brushing his forehead with his hand, "so that I had only my uncles to speak for me before the Wise Ones. But my uncles were both good men.

Both loved me and both belonged to the tribal council, whose members had all counted coup and were leaders. No man can love children more than my people do, and while I missed my father this day more than ever, I knew my uncles looked on me as a son and that they would help me now.

"Both of them were waiting, and when I was ready they led me to the lodge of Yellow-bear, where our chiefs sat with the Wise Ones. When I entered and sat down, Yellow-bear passed the pipe round the lodge, as the sun goes, from east to west. Each man took it as it came, and smoked, first offering the stem to the Sun, the father, and then to the Earth, the mother of all things on this world. But no one spoke. All in that lodge had been over the hard trail and each knew well what was in my heart by my eyes. The eyes of living men speak words which the tongue cannot pronounce. The dead do not see out of their bodies' eyes, because there is no spirit there. It has gone away forever. In the lodge of Yellow-bear that day seventy years ago I saw the spirits [souls] of my leaders in their eyes, and my heart sang loudly because I had dreamed.

"When the pipe was finished, my uncle, White-horse, laid his hand on my shoulder. 'Speak, Plenty-coups,' he said. 'Tell us your dream. Forget nothing that happened. You are too young to understand, but here are men who can help you.' "

At this point a rolling hoop bumped violently against the Chief's chair and fell flat beside it. The old man did not start or show the least displeasure, even when a little bright-eyed girl ran among us to recover it. He did not reprove her with so much as a look. Instead, he smiled. "I have adopted many children," he said softly. Then he went on.

"I told my dream, all of it. Even a part I forgot to tell you, about trying to enter a lodge on my way back from this place to the Crazies. A Voice had spoken. 'Do not go inside,' it said. 'This lodge contains the clothes of small babies, and if you touch them or they touch you, you will not be successful.' Of course I did not enter that lodge, but went on to my bed in the mountains. This I told in the order it came in my dream.

"When I had finished, Yellow-bear, who sat at the head of the lodge which faced the east, lighted the pipe and passed it to his left, as the sun goes. Four times he lit the pipe, and four times it went round the lodge, without a word being spoken by anybody who took it. I grew uneasy. Was there no meaning in my dream?

" 'White-horse,' the voice of Yellow-bear said softly, 'your nephew has dreamed a great dream.'

"My heart began to sing again. Yellow-bear

was the wisest man in the lodge. My ears were listening.

" 'He has been told that in his lifetime the buffalo will go away forever,' said Yellow-bear, 'and that in their place on the plains will come the bulls and the cows and the calves of the white men. I have myself seen these Spotted-buffalo drawing loads of the white man's goods. And once at the big fort above the mouth of the Elk River [Fort Union, above the mouth of the Yellowstone] on the Big River [Missouri] I saw cows and calves of the same tribe as the bulls that drew the loads.

" 'The dream of Plenty-coups means that the white men will take and hold this country and that their Spotted-buffalo will cover the plains. He was told to think for himself, to listen, to learn to avoid disaster by the experiences of others. He was advised to develop his body but not to forget his mind. The meaning of his dream is plain to me. I see its warning. The tribes who have fought the white man have all been beaten, wiped out. By listening as the Chickadee listens we may escape this and keep our lands.

" 'The Four Winds represent the white man and those who will help him in his wars. The forest of trees is the tribes of these wide plains. And the one tree that the Four Winds left standing after the fearful battle represents our own people, the Absarokees, the one tribe of the plains that has never made war against the white man.

" 'The Chickadee's lodge in that standing tree is the lodges of this tribe pitched in the safety of peaceful relations with white men, whom we could not stop even though we would. The Chickadee is small, so are we against our many enemies, white and red. But he was wise in his selection of a place to pitch his lodge. After the battle of the Four Winds he still held his home, his country, because he had gained wisdom by listening to the mistakes of others and knew there was safety for himself and his family. The Chickadee is the medicine of Plenty-coups from this day. He will not be obliged to carry a heavy medicine-bundle, but his medicine will be powerful both in peace time and in war.

" 'He will live to be old and he will be a Chief. He will some day live differently from the way we do now and will sit in the shade of great trees on Arrow Creek, where the Man-person took him in his dream. The old man he saw there was himself, as he was told. He will live to be old and be known for his brave deeds, but I can see that he will have no children of his own blood. This was told him when he tried to enter that lodge on his way from Arrow Creek to the peak in the Crazy Mountains where he dreamed. When the

Voice told him not to enter, that the lodge was filled with the clothes of babes, that if he touched them he would not succeed, it meant he would have no children. I have finished.' "

" 'Your dream was a great dream. Its meaning is plain,' said the others, and the pipe was passed so that I might smoke with them in the lodge of Yellow-bear.

"Ho!" said Plenty-coups, making the sign for "finished." "And here I am, an old man, sitting under this tree just where that old man sat seventy years ago when this was a different world."

Coyote-runs and Plain-bull began a conversation between themselves when Plenty-coups left off talking. Both said that the dream of the Chief was well known to all the tribe, even the day after he had returned from his dreaming. "We traveled by that dream," said Coyote-runs. "The men who sat in that lodge when Plenty-coups told what he had seen and heard knew a heap better than he did that it was time the Crows turned their faces another way. They saw it was best to do something to prove their friendship to white men, and they began to watch for a chance, too. When they found it, the Crows pointed their guns with the white man's, and some of us died and we lost many horses."

"Yes," added Plain-bull, "and the White

Chief never paid us when we were his soldiers, never even paid us for our dead horses."

The sky was darkening in the west, and now thunder muttered. There was a gust of damp wind. A pinto pony, beautifully built, came trotting through the open gate. He was saddled, and the bridle reins were over the saddle-horn, as though he had taken advantage of an opportunity. "The little boy must walk. His horse has left him somewhere," smiled Coyote-runs.

A woman, the wife of the Chief, came through the door of the log house and leaned against the porch support, her eyes on the western sky. She was rather fat. She wore a gingham dress of a faded red color, moccasins, and a red handkerchief tied over her hair, which I saw was a little gray. A lusty gust of damp wind rustled the cottonwood leaves, and the woman stepped off the porch and began industriously to take the red meat from the racks, piling it in her arms until they held all she could stagger under. Then she carried it inside and came out for another load. Magpies scolded her, their black and white plumage ruffling in the breeze. But they might as well have protested to the blackening clouds.

"You will come tomorrow?" asked the Chief, when raindrops began to pelt the leaves over our heads.

"Yes, at eight," I told him.

V

IN the morning the old Chief was ready, waiting with his companions, under the trees. There was no preliminary talking, and the story-telling was resumed, the medicine dream figuring in the beginning.

"I do not know if there have been other tribes who fought with the white men and never against them, as we have done," said Plenty-coups. "Listening, as the Chickadee listens, we saw that those who made war against the white men always failed in the end and lost their lands. Look at the Striped-feathered-arrows [Cheyennes]. Most of them are living where they hate the ground that holds their lodges. They cannot look at the mountains as I can or drink good water as I do every day. Instead of making a treaty with the white men and by it holding their country which they loved, they fought. Ah! how those warriors fought! And lost all, taking whatever the white man would give. And when the hearts of the givers are filled with hate their gifts are small.

"The Cheyenne, and the Sioux who fared a little better, have always been our enemies, but I am sorry for them today. I have fought hard against them in war, with the white man more than once, and often with my own tribe before the white man came. But when I fought with the white man against them it was not because I loved him or because I hated the Sioux and Cheyenne, but because I saw that this was the only way we could keep our lands. Look at our country! It was chosen by my people out of the heart of the most beautiful land on all the world, because we were wise. And it was my dream that taught us the way.

"I am old and am living an unnatural life. I know that I am standing on the brink of the life that nobody knows all about, and I am anxious to go to my Father, Ah-badt-dadt-deah, to live again as men were intended to live, even on this world."

Now, as he so often did when he spoke of his age, he trailed off into moody silence, forgetting us altogether. And this time I felt that the thought of leaving his people in an unsettled condition troubled him far more than his own passing, and that if he could turn time back to the days of his boyhood he would gladly die. His pronunciation of the name of his God in his husky voice impressed me deeply, as that name always does when spoken by an aged Indian.

Ah-badt-dadt-deah literally translated means The-one-who-made-all-things. I have sometimes thought that it is more nearly a term than a name, and that to the Crow the name of his God is unpronounceable, as with some of the ancient peoples. However, the Indian—certainly any that I know—will scarcely ever speak the name of his God aloud; and if you pronounce it in his presence you will feel his reverence. There will be instant silence, and the Indian's attitude will have changed. His God is All, Everywhere; and this is the reason why, in crossing a stream, he will sometimes give the water a bit of fat meat or some little finery. This is not to propitiate evil spirits who live in the water, but it is an offering to the All-high so that the Indian may pass safely through an element that he recognizes as not naturally his own. But if you speak of E-sac-ca-wata (Old-man-coyote), or Napa, or Nu-lach-kin-nah (Old man), a powerful character to whom the Almighty entrusted much of the work of creation, every old Indian will smile. The Indians hold him in no reverence and are ready to laugh at the mention of his name, since it was he who made the seeming mistakes in nature, not the Almighty who commissioned him. This, to me, is a delicious touch, for thus, in his few fault-findings with created things like the elements that sometimes torture, the Indian cannot blaspheme against his God, for whom he holds the deepest reverence. Here, too, I believe is proof that the Indian of this section certainly is a monotheist.

At this point, while arguing over the proper spelling of Ah-badt-dadt-deah with Mr. Frank Shively (Braided-scalp-lock), who is a Carlisle man, our voices became unduly loud. Plenty-coups, hearing the name of his God spoken more than once in this manner, roused himself. "Stop!" he said, sternly. "You must not speak that name in so loud a voice." Then, remembering his story, he went on:

"I have no sons or daughters of my own blood, but instead, as Yellow-bear foretold, all the Crows are my children and I love them as a father. Once my woman believed that in spite of my dream we might have children. She spent moons making a beautiful robe for herself to wear, splitting and perfectly matching two tanned buffalo skins. She painted it to please her fancy and I well remember that while the painting was strange to me the work was very handsome. Besides the robe, she made herself a belt by cutting a narrow strip from a buffalo hide along the back so as to include the tail. Wearing these things, she went often to The-baby-place and spoke secretly to The-little-ones-of-the-pool. She even followed the custom of women who had lived before her and left a bow and four arrows and a hoop and stick by the pool for the Little-ones to play with. But we had no children that lived. Two were born, but both died."

We were interrupted by the white man who had been mowing the Chief's hay. This fellow always addressed the Chief as "Mister Plenty-coups," but of course spoke through an interpreter. While he told his wants, I thought of The-baby-place. I had visited it. It is not far from Pryor. From the house of Plenty-coups one can see the rocks that hide it. The sandstone rim above Arrow Creek juts out and overhangs a tiny pool of water which rises and falls with the streams of the district. It is roofed by the rock above it and is completely concealed by surrounding bushes, so that unless one knew its exact location he would not find it. During the summer and fall when the pool is low it has a smooth muddy shoreline that leads into a shadowy cave at the back. In this soft little beach Crow women who expected babies often saw the tiny footprints of The-little-ones-of-the-pool, a boy and a girl who dwelt there in eternal childhood and who possessed the power to tell coming Crow mothers the sex of their unborn children. To learn if her child would be a son or a daughter the Crow woman secretly made a bow and four arrows: one red, one blue, one black, and one yellow. Besides these she made a hoop and a stick and placed them all on the little beach beside the pool, leaving them undisturbed for four nights and four days. If, when she returned, the bow and arrows were gone she knew her child would be a boy, that his spirit had taken the mimic weapons to play with. A girl would have taken the hoop and stick.

The story of the discovery of The-baby-place is very old. I made notes on it long ago. I was wondering what I had done with them when the white man who ran the mowing machine went away, leaving the Chief to go on with his story.

"When my woman died," he said, as though he had not been diverted, "I married her sister, but there were no children born to us. Everything foretold by my great dream has come to pass. All through my life I have seen *signs* that told me to go ahead, that all would be according to my dream.

"The first sign I saw was twelve years after I had dreamed in the Crazies. There was a fog over the plains, and the mountains were completely hidden by it. Even the sun was dim in the sky. My eyes could look long at him that day, and I saw that he was like a war-shield bearing two scalps. The hair of one was braided and long, of the other loose and shorter. Both were blowing in the wind that was stirring far above the fog. And the war-shield was my own! Its painting was the same as mine!

"Yellow-crow was with me, and we were near The-fasting-place that white men call Square Butte. 'Look!' I said, pointing up to dim sun. 'Look, and tell me what you see.'

" 'Your shield!' he said, surprised. 'And there are two scalps on it!' I knew then that I should soon take the scalps of two enemies; and I did. I have taken many. My first and second were the riders of the *white* and *black* horses, counted in the dream-lodge by the Chief of the Dwarfs.

"But in all my life I have never killed a white man. They have stolen my horses often, and I have stolen them back without killing the white thieves. I have even captured white men for their own chiefs more than once. What their chiefs did with them I do not know. But I did not harm them myself, even though they had killed some of my people."

I knew that the laws of most tribes of the plains permit a man to choose the sister of his deceased wife, no matter how other suitors may feel. Plenty-coups said that he had taken the sister of his late wife, and I questioned him. He told me that he had married several times, and I learned that upon the death of his late wife her sister, who is his present companion, left a husband to come and live with Plenty-coups, according to ancient custom. "It was our way, but our young people are leaving custom behind them. They marry anybody they choose, whether fit or not," he said.

What a life he has seen, I thought, looking into his strong wide face, seamed and almost pale compared with Plain-bull's. I tried to turn him back to talk of his childhood, to get him started on some incident that would show more of the life of an Indian boy seventy-five years ago. But he laughed at my suggestions. "We played at being men," he said, as though I knew all about it.

"I am sure I shall not be able to tell you things in their order," he went on. "I shall get things behind that ought to be ahead. Just now I am thinking of the summer I became eleven years old. From early springtime until the snows fell there was something new and stirring each day, and the summer was very fine. Meat was fat and plentiful when the days began to grow shorter. Ripe plums were thick on the trees, and black chokecherries bent the bushes with their weight.

"One night in the early spring of that year, when our village was near The-mountain-lion's-lodge [Pompey's Pillar], a young warrior named Bear-in-the-water had a dream. In it he saw a camp of Flatheads far to the westward. Many horses were tied near their lodges, some of them our own. One horse was chestnut with a light-colored belly. He looked very fast. Anyhow he was a handsome horse, and Bear-in-the-water wished to possess him. When he told his dream, thirty-five of us young men agreed to go with him to steal the chestnut horse and as many others as we could. We had a score to settle with the Flatheads anyway.

"We elected Bear-in-the-water to carry the pipe [to be leader], and very early next morning we set out toward our leader's dream-camp, crossing Elk River and following it upstream. We came out of the high hills near the present site of the city of Bozeman, and later on reached the three forks of the Big River. Here our Wolves brought us news. They had seen elk moving as though disturbed and had heard a gun.

While they were telling us this, two more Wolves came in and told us more. These two had been on a high hill and had seen Flathead hunters packing elk meat on horses. They said the valley ahead was very good to look at and that there were rivers everywhere.

"Of course we knew the camp of the Flatheads which Bear-in-the-water had seen in his dream was not far away now, and at once got ready for action by hiding everything we had with us, which was not much of a task. We left Bear-in-the-water with our things, because he had brought his woman along with us to do our cooking, and somebody must guard our horses and robes. But he would not stay until we promised him the chestnut horse if we got him.

"The sun was in the middle of the sky, and black clouds were gathering when twenty-five of us started out to locate the Flathead camp, while nine men went searching for the loose horses belonging to the enemy. But when we found it we could not count the lodges because of the heavy rain that had begun to fall almost as soon as we started. We were obliged to wait for night anyway, and when it came it was unusually dark, with rain as cold as snow.

"We scattered and began moving in, each man for himself. I kept looking at the lodge-fires through the driving rain that pelted my naked back, trying to count them as I crawled nearer and nearer.

"Suddenly I heard laughing. It was loud and came from a dark lodge I could almost touch. I was in the camp without knowing it, and stopped to look around me. There were three dark objects not far behind, and I knew they were Crows. Only four of us had come to the camp! The others must have gone round it to try to stampede the loose horses, I knew. But would they wait long enough for me to cut a horse?

"The rain had grown a little finer now, and I could see between twenty and thirty lodge-fires ahead. I crept on, and soon there were lodges all around me, and I could smell fresh elk meat everywhere. The Flatheads were living high. I wondered how many of their men were asleep.

"At last I stood up and moved forward between two lodges, the rain coming again in torrents, shutting out all but the blur of a few lodge-fires. I thought of the men who had gone round the camp to stampede the loose horses. I must hurry.

"Something bumped against me! The thing struck my thigh and was hard and cold. I put down my hand to feel it. A rope! My fingers closed around it, and I got down on my hands and knees to follow it up, to learn where it led, and what it was tied to. I crept along the rope till I came to a deep puddle of water. When I stopped to find a way around it I saw something black just behind me and it moved! I bent lower, my eyes straining to make out what the black thing was, when a voice whispered, 'I am with you.'

"I knew it was Big-horn who spoke. 'Wait where you are,' I whispered, and began again to follow my rope till it led me to a horse. At last I had a chance, but just as I rose up to cut his rope a man stepped out of a lodge right behind me, almost on Big-horn.

"I sank my body to the ground and waited, with my hand still on the rope. The man had left his lodge door open, and I could see into the lodge. A woman sat by the fire, but I saw no children near her. The lodge was neat. The man merely looked at the weather a little, and as soon as he had gone back into the lodge I cut the rope. There was little time to spare, I knew, and I got out of there as fast as I could lead my horse. Not even a dog spoke, and outside the camp I ran on to Big-horn and the two others I had seen when I was entering the Flathead camp. 'This is foolish,' I said. 'We cannot see in this rain. Let us get away from here.'

" 'Listen!' Big-horn whispered.

"Horses were coming! We four hurried to our hiding place as fast as we could go, reaching it just as the others came in with a large band of loose horses. Not a shot had been fired, no Flathead dog had spoken, and we were merry over our good luck, though quiet about it. Whoever carried the pipe for that Flathead camp was a careless man.

"At daybreak we looked at our stolen property, and there, sure enough, was the chestnut horse with the light-colored belly, the horse of Bear-in-the-water's dream. He took him, of course; but my horse, the one I had cut in the camp, was a mule! I had seen one or two mules before, but in the black darkness and rain I had not known what I was getting. There was blood on his back, and by this we knew how he came to be tied to a man's lodge like a war-horse. They had been using the mule to pack meat and would need him again in the morning. But he wouldn't be there!

"Bear-in-the-water told us the Flatheads had many guns and plenty of powder and balls. We had but four guns and very little ammunition for them, so that we must get ready for trouble. Six of us were sent to a high hill to learn what the Flatheads were doing and to count their lodges. I was one of the six.

"The rain had now ceased falling, but the clouds were yet heavy with it, and more might come down any time. We hurried, but before we were halfway up the hill a shot rang out below us. It sounded as though it had been fired near our hiding place. There was no good in going farther. Our party had been discovered, it was plain, and we raced down again with plenty of shots popping in the vicinity of our hiding place. And our party was retreating into the timber. We soon saw the Crows, driving the stolen horses ahead of them, disappear among the trees, and I was astonished at the number of the enemy. We learned afterward that there were fifty lodges in their camp.

"Many of their warriors were between us and the Crows, and we must ride for it, go through them, to reach our friends. Bending low over our horses' necks we dashed for the timber in a sudden downpour of heavy rain that hid us a little but made us blind. Two arrows whizzed near my ear, and a bullet that had struck something cried like a crippled rabbit over my head, but we reached the timber untouched.

"Not a Crow was in sight there, nor a horse. Our friends had got away with the stolen band, but we six were in a bad situation. There were Flatheads all around us in the timber, and our horses would hamper our escape. We sprang from their backs and left them, scattering out, each for himself, dodging away among the trees, expecting to be stopped by an enemy.

"Twice I saw the trail of the stolen horses, but both times there were Flatheads between them and me, and I dared not follow it. Running on, my eyes everywhere, I caught sight of Goes-against-the-enemy beckoning me from behind a tree, and went to him. He had found a white man's log cabin and led us all to it. White trappers had built it the year before, and it would keep us dry while we planned a way out of our difficulties. But no sooner had the door closed, shutting us in the dark, than I thought I saw a Flathead through a crack between the logs. My eyes had just caught him when he moved under a big tree back of the cabin, and I held up my hand for silence. The five stood still as stones while I put my eyes to that crack.

"Yes, he was there, right enough, with his back against the tree—a big man with a gun, and very wet. He had on a white blanket capote from the Hudson's Bay people up north and, if the crack had been wide enough, was a fine mark. But it was not, and all I could do was look at him standing still as the big tree itself. When at last he turned his head I looked the way he did, and saw two more Flatheads slipping toward the cabin, one with a gun. Had they seen us enter? Were they closing in on us, I wondered.

"I turned around to tell my companions, but used to the light outside, my eyes were blind and

I did not know that Big-horn, who had our only gun, had been looking too, until he opened the door and stepped out.

"Instantly, before he could even raise his gun, a Flathead bullet smashed his right arm from the wrist to the shoulder, burying itself deep in his armpit. I dragged him inside and shut the door. He was bleeding badly, and I saw that it would be difficult to stop the blood because of the wound under his arm. But we tried, while bullets smacked against the cabin logs, some of them coming through between the cracks so that we had to move Big-horn several times while we worked on him.

"If we stayed in the cabin they could starve or burn us out, even if they did not take the place by fighting. We had but the one gun, and had come near losing that. Our bows could not be used unless we went outside to fight, and the Flatheads were too many for us. Big-horn, leaning against the logs, clearly understood our situation. 'You had better get out of this place,' he said. 'I shall die anyway, and you cannot help me by dying yourselves. I am no good any more.'

"He was my friend. 'No,' I told him. 'I will not leave you.'

" 'Nor will I,' said Goes-against-the-enemy. 'But the rest had better go if they can. Three had better die than six.'

"'Yes, go,' I begged them. And so they stepped out into the pouring rain in the face of the Flatheads.

"We watched them through the cracks, even Big-horn, as long as we could see them, until the dripping bushes hid them. Then for a long time we scarcely breathed, listening for shots. But none reached our ears, and we three were in for a hard time, we well knew.

"There was no longer any good in silence. The Flatheads knew we were in the cabin as well as we did, but they did not know that three of our party had got out of their trap. Wishing them to know we were ready to die, we defied them with the Crow war whoop. Then we sang our Death Song and waited.

"It was now that we tried again to stop Big-horn's blood, but in spite of all we could do he continued to bleed. Not so badly, but enough to warn us that he could not last long. He was aware of this and said, 'I can travel. Let us get out of this place when night comes. It is not far off now, and perhaps we may find our friends.' He even laughed a little at my serious look when I tried to twist the thongs tighter about his upper arm.

"I expected the Flatheads would burn the cabin when night came. I knew the logs would burn in spite of all the rain. The flames might not reach us for a time, and we might get good shots at our enemy in their light, but the smoke would not let us live very long. I counted the bullets in Big-horn's pouch—eleven. Not many to make a fight with, but better than none if we could keep the door open. 'Let us get out of this place,' urged Big-horn, when I put the string of his bullet pouch over my own head and took his gun.

" 'If he thinks he can travel we had better try,' said Goes-against-the-enemy. And I agreed.

"Dark came early. The rain was still falling when we three crept out of the cabin. Goes-against-the-enemy was ahead, Big-horn and I behind with the gun. Not once did we stop to look or listen. There was nothing one could see, and the rain stopped every small sound from going very far. Our great danger was that we might creep right in among the Flatheads who were watching the cabin, but we went swiftly over fallen trees and among bushes that showered our backs with water held in their young leaves, till we reached a creek. Here Goes-against-the-enemy stood up to wade across, and I helped Big-horn to stand. His head struck a leaning alder tree, and he staggered into my arms just as a gun flashed in our faces. I saw Big-horn's eyes in its light. They were dead.

"Holding him from falling I led him into the

water, expecting to be killed. But we got across, and dropping back to our hands and knees followed Goes-against-the-enemy, who was just ahead, until we came to another creek. This time I lifted Big-horn to his feet and saw that he was bleeding worse than when we left the cabin. 'Can you walk across?' I asked him.

" 'No,' he said. 'I can go no farther. I am finished. Leave me and run.' He sank down at my feet, and Goes-against-the-enemy, who had already crossed the creek, came back. 'Sit down beside me,' whispered Big-horn, 'and sing with me while I go to my Father.'

"We sat down and sang there in the rain. And he sang with us until his heart was still. Big-horn, my friend, was dead in the enemy's country. My heart was on the ground beside him.

"We gave him the best things we had, my necklace of bear's teeth and Goes-against-the-enemy's belt of porcupine quills, that he might offer them to our Father, and we left him lying on a bed we made in the dark. But we carefully covered him with willows so that the Flatheads should not find him, nor the wolves disturb his body.

" 'When we come back to get him, if we live to come,' I said to Goes-against-the-enemy, 'we will sing of his deeds and ask his spirit to stay always with us, as we stayed with him when he was here.'

" 'Yes,' he answered, 'we will do as you say, and now let us make our hearts sing because our friend died unafraid.'

"Though we could travel faster now, there were many grizzly bears to trouble us. We ran close to them often. I did not like to meet so many in the darkness, but we kept on until morning came. The sight of the trail of the stolen horses lightened our hearts a little, but we were tired and hungry, needing rest and food. We killed a deer and camped on a high hill where we could look east and west, slept like stones, by turns, and took up the trail of the horses at daybreak. I could run from sun to sun in those days, and we ran most of the time till we caught up with our friends.

"I have forgotten to tell you that we lost the trail where two rivers join their waters and that a Crow waiting on the bluff told us with a buffalo robe to follow the right-hand stream. I was glad to see that man and just as glad to get back to our village, which was then on Arrow Creek. It was much larger than when we left it, near The-mountain-lion's-lodge, because the clans had gathered to plant the tobacco-seed."

## VI

I INTERRUPTED here to beg Plenty-coups to tell me about the ceremony of planting the tobacco-seed, which originated in a dream and is very old. He was willing enough, as other old men have been, and until he came to tell how the chief actor in the ceremony, a woman, is appointed, I made notes. Then, as has happened before when I tried to get this ceremony straight in my mind, I could not understand and questioned further. Twice the old man went over the puzzling points, and twice I was obliged to admit my inability to grasp them. "Ho!" he said, suddenly dropping the whole question. "There is Something here! Something that does not wish you to understand. Do not try, Sign-talker. Let it alone."

Urging him was useless. I should like to understand this Crow ceremony thoroughly and record it. I can give no clear picture from my present knowledge of it. Each year the Crows plant the seed in carefully prepared and fertilized ground with an elaborate ceremony that it may flourish and the tribe experience a prosperous season. The seed is not of the tobacco plant, and is said by the Crows to be deadly poison, even capable of causing skin eruptions through careless handling. I long ago sent samples of the seed to our State University, but not yet have I learned its true name or source. I believe that it may have originally come from the South. The Crows are loath to part with any of it, and for that reason I found a little difficulty in obtaining it. While in my possession it did not cause skin eruptions, because, I have been told by Crows, I have a "right" to handle it.

"Did you go back for Big-horn's body?" I asked, to help him pick up his story.

"We entered the village quietly because of the loss of Big-horn," he said, as though this was not the proper time to answer my question. "I dreaded the mourning of his family more than

I can make you believe. I had gone with the party to help even up some old scores, and now, although we had many of their horses, I had another and a stronger reason for going again against the Flatheads. They had killed my friend.

"Before we could tell our story the people missed Big-horn. His father cut off a finger, and both he and his woman, the mother of Big-horn, slashed their bodies with knives and wailed pitifully. Of course none of his close relatives could now enter the ceremony of planting the tobacco-seed, and all those who continued the preparations for it felt sad.

"Big-horn had four fine war-horses. Before telling the story of our raid against the Flatheads we cut their tails short and roached their manes. 'I will go back and fetch the body of Big-horn to his people,' I promised his father, and I knew I should not rest until this was accomplished.

"No members of our war-party took part in the planting of the seed, each of us instead taking a sweat-bath and fasting through the day and night. When morning came and the rest were beginning the beautiful ceremony, we painted our faces black, mounted our best war-horses, and rode away upon the knolls.

"Each man was by himself, with his horse. There were thirty-four of us on thirty-four high points that looked down into the village. We neither ate nor drank water, but gave our thoughts to Big-horn, our brother, who was gone. To be alone with our war-horses at such a time teaches them to understand us, and us to understand them. My horse fights with me and fasts with me, because if he is to carry me in battle he must know my heart and I must know his or we shall never become brothers. I have been told that the white man, who is almost a god, and yet a great fool, does not believe that the horse has a spirit [soul]. This cannot be true. I have many times seen my horse's soul in his eyes. And this day on that knoll I knew my horse understood. I saw his soul in his eyes.

"Down in the village I saw the planters start for the planting place, saw the people crowd too close to them, watched, only half perceiving, the War-clubs push them back. One man picked up a snake to strike those who were too near the sacred line of planters. I heard the singing as these people started, saw them stop, then start again, singing toward the planting ground. I felt glad that the seed would be planted, but my heart was not with the planters. It was on the ground in the enemy's country with Big-horn.

"The next morning the village moved to Yellow-willows [Sage Creek] but did not stop there long, because our Wolves signalled us from the high hills that there were many buffalo on the Stinking Water. The tribe moved there and began to hunt.

"But I could not rest, and so when the village moved to the Rapids [Rock Creek] I gathered five of my best friends and told them I proposed going after the body of Big-horn. When they said they would go with me my heart felt like a breath-feather.

"We made panniers of rawhide large enough to carry Big-horn, put them on the back of a strong horse, and started, traveling all that day and night. On the third day we reached a country where we must not be seen, and after this moved only at night. One morning, just as we were hiding for the day, we heard a shot and raced for a high hill to learn who fired it. Goes-against-the-enemy beat us all to the top. I was nearest when he sprang from his horse and looked over the hill. By the time I had reached him he was up again and had signalled 'The enemy is here.' Then he mounted and dashed down on the far side out of sight.

"I got off my horse and looked over the hill. One mounted Flathead was in sight, a fine-looking man, too. He wore on his head a rawhide hat and carried a beautiful gun. I saw its brass patch-box flashing in the sunlight. But it was a very heavy weapon, so heavy the Flathead carried two rest-sticks for it. I held up my hand and stopped our party quite a way down the hill. The Flathead rightfully belonged to Goes-against-the-enemy, who had seen him first, and I wished him to have his chance.

"When our party stopped I watched Goes-against-the-enemy. He was riding very near the Flathead before the fellow saw him at all. The Flathead raised his heavy gun, fitting his rest-sticks against his side, and fired just as Goes-against-the-enemy struck him in the face with his quirt. I heard the lash strike, a beautiful coup!

"I waited no longer, but jumped upon my horse and raced down the hill to count coup myself. I would take the Flathead's gun. Watching Goes-against-the-enemy, who had turned his horse to come back, he was trying to reload it. He had not seen me. His horse was running at right angles to my course, and my horse ran into his so violently that both nearly fell. But on the instant of collision I grabbed the Flathead's gun and held on, trying desperately to pull him from his horse. We wrestled, riding across the level ground as fast as our unmanaged horses could run, both holding to the gun, each trying to pull the other from his horse, and thus holding the racing animals together as though tied. Though I soon began to tire, I dared not let go. Where was Goes-against-the-enemy, I wondered. My arms were aching as though they must have rest, or break. I must end things somehow.

"So with a last desperate effort I pulled the Flathead nearly over. His head was against my breast, and I pressed down, down, my eyes looking for friends. They saw none, but they saw something else that made my heart sink—the Flathead camp! We were racing straight for it.

" 'Shoot! Shoot!' I cried out, not knowing if friend or foe could hear me.

" 'Lean far over, quick!' The voice was Big-shield's.

"My heart sang again. But though I tried to lean over, the Flathead was a strong man and I could not hold myself away from him enough so that Big-shield's bullet would hit him and not me.

" 'Push him away from you! Push him away!' Big-shield yelled. 'I'll kill him when you do.'

"But I could not push him away. The Flathead, who knew just what was going on, hugged me to himself as we flew toward the camp of his friends.

"Another Crow now came with advice. Whipping his horse to reach us, he was just behind Big-shield when he shouted, 'Do not shoot! Be wise, and hold your arrow!' It was Shot-in-the-hand. 'We are discovered,' he said. 'We are in their village and must make peace if we can.'

"I believed his advice was good. The Flathead was more than I could handle, and I let go. So did he. I believe he was glad of the chance. I know I was. That Flathead was a good man, a good warrior, but a little careless.

"Shot-in-the-hand spoke to the Flathead in the Nez Perce tongue, and he understood. He knew we could easily kill him now, and he expected us to do it, I think. I wished to, myself, but in a way we had made peace, and when Long-Shoshone, who carried our pipe, came up, we took the Flathead to his lodge.

"We were well enough off, but had we known there were only four lodges in the camp we might easily have avenged Big-horn while I still had hold of the Flathead. As it was we ate the meat of his people, and all the time I was in their camp I was sorry I had tasted it. However, there would come another time, and then there would be no peace between them and me. Goes-against-the-enemy felt the same as I did.

"After leaving their camp we did not trust the Flatheads, traveling at night and each day putting out Wolves to watch the elk and buffalo. These animals are always quick to tell a war-party if the enemy is near. But we saw nothing, not even the smoke of an enemy's fire, and at last came to Big-horn's body. It had not been disturbed, and we carried it back with us to the Crow country, finding our village on the spot where Park City now stands."

After much urging by my interpreter and myself the Chief had reluctantly given me the names of two men who had played leading parts with him in the raid against the Flatheads. I felt satisfied, but asked, "Can you remember the names of the men who made up that war-party against the Flatheads?"

"It is not good to speak them or try to count them," he replied. "Each time we do this there is another gone."

They are sworn to secrecy. The plains Indian, even the most willing story-teller, is restrained by deep respect for tribal customs and a way of thinking not comprehensible to the white man. A war-party resolved itself into a secret society at its first camping place, where each member confessed deeds never mentioned elsewhere. Its members were sworn to die for one another if need be.

Such custom hampers. In attempting to trace a family tree, or relationship, one soon learns that an old Indian of the plains will never speak the name of his mother-in-law. This is forbidden; neither will he speak to her himself, nor will she address him. If she happens to be in his lodge visiting her daughter, his wife, when he enters, she covers her face with her robe and immediately leaves. This is the old law. Some tribes, in making the sign for "mother-in-law" make "ashamed," or "hidden-face." Many of the names I have used in this book were obtained from younger men than Plenty-coups, who refused to speak them.

My question had raised up old faces, I think, since for a long time after answering he spoke not a word but silently puffed his pipe. These moments gave me opportunity to study his own face, which changed readily with his moods from mirth to sadness, the latter oftenest betraying his thoughts. But it could be stern—was naturally so—could keep its dignity in any presence, and, defying age, belie a mirthful or sad heart.

"We were now beginning to get more guns," he said, as though he had just returned to us from a distance. "We traded furs and robes to the white traders for them. But it was a long time before we saw a breech-loading gun. I do not believe they were yet made in the day I speak of. When they finally came I did not rest until I owned one, giving ten finely dressed robes for it. Such a gun could be loaded on a running horse, and I laid my bow away forever. But some of the older men stuck tight to their familiar weapon. I could understand why they did so before the cartridge gun came, but after that the bow seemed only a plaything. Sometimes a man would lose his gun or trade it away, and then for a time he would be obliged to go back to his bow and arrows; but we younger men got guns and kept them. They evened things with our enemies, who had had them long before we did. They are noisy weapons, and in the days of the muzzle-loaders, powder was always getting wet.

"The Sioux, Cheyennes, and Arapahoes were often combined against us, so that we were greatly outnumbered, as I have said, and almost constantly fighting to hold our country. This condition kept us all alert and our Wolves especially suspicious of everything that moved on the plains. It led to mistakes too. I made one myself.

"I had just joined the Foxes and was very anxious to distinguish myself as a member. This day the society was policing the village, and I had been sent to a high hill, not only to watch the enemy, but also to prevent young men from slipping out to go to war by themselves. I had often been obliged to dodge the Foxes or the War-clubs in order to get out myself, and I did not intend to let any young man get past me, now that I was a Fox-man on duty. I had a telescope and a good gun, the air was very clear, and

I could see a long way; so that everything was as it should be to help me keep my watch. I did not believe a thing could escape my eyes. For a long time they saw nothing. But when the wind changed a little I saw smoke rising up on Lodge-grass, and with my glass made out a large Sioux and Cheyenne village. The enemy was in our country and would attack us, or at least steal some horses.

"I now had news to signal the Foxes in the village, and stood up with a robe; but I let it fall without saying what I had intended. Horses were coming—many of them—driven by three men who were coming toward the village!

" 'The enemy is coming!' I signalled. Then I mounted my horse to meet the three Sioux. My start gave me advantage over the warriors who, as soon as my signal was seen, had sprung upon their ponies and were coming behind me. But the enemy turned out to be three young Crows who had slipped out of our village and stolen a band of the enemy's horses in broad daylight. The joke was on me. For a long time the Foxes teased me over my signal 'The enemy is coming.'

"Of course we could only smile, now that the thing was done, but how those young men got out of that village without being seen remains a mystery to this day. I never felt the least resentment against them, although they had made a fool of me, but felt glad over their accomplishment. Success, attained by the same act that would lead failure to punishment, too often meets praise."

He stopped, evidently pondering over his last sentence, and, feeling for his tobacco pouch, filled his stone pipe. "Those three young men fooled me, and years passed before I heard the last of my signal 'The enemy is coming,' " he said again, more to his pipe than to me.

"What good days they were, when I was young!" he went on. There was more real merriment now in his face than I had yet seen. "It was about this time that I discovered a large boat on the Big River. I had heard of boats, and now I saw a very large one loaded heavily with white men's goods going up the river to some fort. Frenchmen, who sang happily, pulled it along with the largest rope I had ever seen, but in spite of the pads stuffed with antelope hair, I noticed that every man's shoulders were sore. All one day I watched them, riding along to see them pass the big rope around trees on the bank, and keep the boat going steadily. Their work was hard and they traveled slowly. I feel sure I could have walked three times as far as they dragged that boat, in half the time. But the Frenchmen sang almost constantly, as though they were glad.

"Afterward I saw that same boat coming back

down the river with furs and robes. And now, when the river itself was doing all the work and there was reason for gladness, nobody on the boat was singing. I never understood this."

The old Chief stood up and, at first in pantomime, gave me a perfect picture of the laboring Frenchmen, bending to an imaginary rope over his shoulder. Then, timed to his staggering steps, he sang a little. But his music was not so good. He sang not French but Crow.

It was no wonder the keel-boat had impressed the young Plenty-coups. These boats were often seventy feet long and regularly built, not flat-bottomed but round, with a keel. They were cordelled up the streams, as Plenty-coups had described, though sometimes in crossing or in navigating shallows and swift water, poles were used. The Frenchmen, fitting the pole ends beneath their arms and walking aft, pushed the pole against the bottom. At times a sail was used and occasionally oars, but cordelling was the usual means of propulsion, and from twelve to twenty miles was considered a day's journey. The keel-boat was extensively used down to the late thirties and did not entirely disappear until much later, when steamboats became common on the Missouri.

## VII

"I AM skipping things because I have forgotten them," Plenty-coups said, "but perhaps they are not worth remembering. You have asked me if I could tell you anything about the ring of stones on the top of the bluff above Billings. No, I know nothing about it. It was always there. That spot is big medicine. Once, before my time, a band of our people were camped near it and smallpox broke out among them, nearly wiping them out. They did not then know what this sickness was and they were frightened. Two young warriors who had sweethearts in the village, to save them from the sickness, mounted a snow-white horse, and singing their Death Songs, rode double over the bluff to their deaths. They fell almost where the large building stands today [Midland Fair-Ground building]. We call it The-place-of-skulls generally, although some have named it The-place-where-the-white-horse-went-down. My uncle told me that the smallpox ceased its torment on the day the two young men rode over the bluff."

Plenty-coups could fix no date for this visitation of smallpox. It was probably in 1837, when the disease was brought to Fort Union above the mouth of the Yellowstone in the steamboat *Saint Peter,* belonging to the American Fur Company. It destroyed many thousands of Indians—estimates differing widely, from 60,000 to 150,000—but I believe both figures exaggerate, though the loss of life was indeed terrible. There was an earlier scourge of smallpox, about 1800, but this could scarcely have been the time referred to by Plenty-coups, who appeared to know nothing about it. Nobody can tell the extent of this first epidemic, but it is known that its toll was very heavy. The sweat-bath, followed by the cold plunge into an icy stream, brought instant death to these sufferers, who for every ill resorted to the sweat-lodge.

The morning that had promised so splendidly darkened before noon, and finally rain drove us into the house. The Chief's dwelling place has two rather large rooms on the ground floor, and I think three rooms upstairs. The living room is also a sleeping apartment and kitchen, having two or three iron beds, a cookstove, a table, and cupboards. The other room on the first floor has a fine fireplace but is otherwise unfurnished and bare. The red meat which the woman had carried in the day before was piled on a wagon-sheet spread in the middle of the floor, with a child's rag doll beside it. There were no curtains, no pictures, no floor coverings; and there was not much light on a dark day. Upstairs the rooms were ceiled with pine, and except for an iron bedstead with bare springs, unfurnished as though just finished. The Chief's was the only two-story house in that country.

Plenty-coups unlocked a door and let me enter his private room where in boxes he has stored his keepsakes of the years. Pictures, photographs, Crow finery, a weapon or two, letters from prominent men he has met, including a President of the United States, generals, and statesmen—little enough, and yet so precious that they are kept under lock and key. In this room a narrow strip of rag carpet leads from the door to the back wall where a bright-colored chromo hangs, and along its other walls are framed photographs of prominent tribesmen long dead. Taken at

Washington, when the men were members of some tribal delegation, these pictures show Indians dressed for a great occasion.

Somehow the room oppressed me, and I was glad when we moved to another, utterly without furniture. We fetched chairs from downstairs. On the wall of this room was a medicine-bundle whose half-exposed contents set me wishing I might possess it. It contained the stuffed skin of a Richardson weasel, the killer of prairie-dogs, now nearly extinct and little known. I was aware, of course, that there was no possibility of obtaining it and so said nothing about the compartment's only adornment, but during the afternoon while the rain pattered on the shingled roof my eyes were often on the giant weasel, whose head and shoulders stuck so engagingly out of the sack. And my thoughts kept reminding me that here in all this apparent poverty, dwelt the Chief of the Crows in the only two-story log house owned by an Indian so far as I know—an example to his people.

Nor had the coat he wore been made for him or bought new by him. It was old and badly worn, its cuffs frayed and its buttons gone. But reflecting upon the chiefs I had known, I realized that there had never been one who was very well off. Poverty was part of a chief's obligations, it has always seemed to me.

He had spoken little since entering the house. Perhaps he was as much oppressed by its interior as I was. I would try to get him started again. The scar on his chin had always interested me. I had noticed it, too, in a photograph he had given me in his private room, and I realized it must be old, because the picture had been taken when he was young.

"The scar on my chin?" he laughed, his deep chest giving power to his merriment. "Plain-bull was with me when I got it, and I was with him when his head was split open. You can see his scar, too, which put him to sleep a long time. It is worse than mine. I thought him dead.

"One cold day in winter we were packing in buffalo meat on a horse not yet broken to ride. He got away from me and let me have both hind feet. They broke my jaw, so that after spitting out most of my teeth on the snow, I was obliged to tie it together to hold it up where it belonged. It would not stay any place and kept falling down. I had to drink soup for more than a moon, but excepting that scar and a place on my side where a bullet burned me, I have no marks on my body that I did not make myself. I have been lucky. My medicine is very strong.

"That was a bad blow that broke Plain-bull's skull. We were packing in meat, and the horses were heavily laden. Plain-bull was behind them and struck one with his quirt. The lash wound round the horse's leg, and when he kicked viciously to free it he pulled Plain-bull to him by the quirt-lash, so that the blow of his hoofs was fair and full. Plain-bull knew nothing at all for two days and nights, yet he sits here with us to-day, as good as ever. We had many accidents when we were young, but we were always happy."

He stopped to smoke. Somehow, indoors, I could not get him going. There were too many interruptions. First the white man came to ask what to do with some horses. Then the rain brought callers who were looking for shelter more than for company, and these sat to listen awhile, often diverting the Chief.

"When did you marry?" I asked, when at last our party was alone in the little room.

"I might have married before I did," he replied. "The young woman I loved was gone forever, and I did not care for any other. I remained single for a long time after I had counted coup. All my companions were married. I mean all that were under twenty-five and had counted coup. There were some, however, who had been unlucky and had not yet married because they had not the right.

"I have seen such young men suffer great bodily pain to gain strength of will to succeed in distinguishing themselves so that they might marry. Sometimes they would get a Wise One to make two clean cuts with a sharp knife on their backs over each shoulder blade, and lift the flesh and skin so that narrow thongs of stout rawhide could be tied to them. With these they dragged heavy loads over the plains all day in the burning sun until dusk, or until their flesh broke and relieved them of their loads. Four dried skulls of buffalo bulls, or the green head [freshly killed] of a large bull that had shown much fight were the usual loads. When the latter was used the skin was left on the head, together with a strip that included the bull's tail. Another drag was the head and hide of a large grizzly bear, and this was a very heavy load. But the heavier the better, because the flesh would break quickest under a hard pull. I always pitied these young men and wished always to help them; but once they assumed the ordeal nobody might offer them aid until the sun set or their flesh broke. Then only a Wise One might help them by first relieving them of their drags (if they had not already been left somewhere on the plains) and dressing their wounded backs."

Somehow, here I was reminded of the little boy with only one good arm who had yesterday told the Chief that the meat was cooked. "Why did young men not marry until twenty-five or until they had counted coup?" I asked Plenty-coups.

"Because a man who has counted coup or one who has reached the age of twenty-five is strong and healthy," he replied. "We breed our horses with great care even today, but we have forgotten ourselves in this respect. Now any man may marry any woman whenever he can. No law prevents this, and sometimes imperfectly formed children are born. I never heard of a deformed child when I was young."

He then told of the old law governing marriage. No man might marry a woman belonging to the same clan as his own, but instead must choose a mate from another clan. Children always belonged to the clan of their mother, and this prevented the possibility of in-breeding, because when they grew up and married they must mate with those of another group. Besides, occasionally there was new blood brought to the Crows from other tribes, so that the race did not decline. He spoke in high praise of the law that permitted men to marry under twenty-five if they had counted coup. "This rule," he said, "made us strive to be strong and brave, and a man can be neither without health." But even though the law permitted a man who had reached the age of twenty-five years and had not counted coup to take a wife, he might not "paint his woman's face;" so that even here tribal distinction was withheld, and the incentive to bravery kept to the fore. "Nothing was finer than to see a pretty young woman with her face painted, riding ahead of her man," said Plenty-coups. "She looked so proud and happy, carrying his lance and shield, riding his best war-horse, to tell everybody that *her* man was a warrior who had distinguished himself in battle. The way of all young men was alike, and difficult. Most of them turned out to be able."

I knew that a young man was always hazed by his older companions on his first war-party, but had little hope that the Chief would tell me what happened to him on *his* first expedition. "What did they do to you on your first war-party?" I suggested. "Did they make fun of you?"

"Yes," he smiled. "I shall always remember my first war-party. I was asked to go by the man who was to carry the pipe, and I felt so proud I could scarcely keep the secret to myself. I thought the day very long, and was relieved when at night we rode silently out of the village with our faces toward the east. We wore only light shirts and leggings made from the skins of big-horns, and carried nothing except our bows and shields. War-bonnets and bright colors were hidden away, because they can be seen easily, and no war-party wishes to be seen. Bonnets were never used by warriors until all chance of surprise was gone. Then they were brought out, if there was time. Our bonnets were in rawhide cases and might not be used at all.

"We rode all night without my seeing our Wolves. Yet I knew, of course, they were out ahead of us somewhere. I kept looking at every knoll top until we hid away for the day. Then they came in, looking exactly like wolves. Each had had mud ears, and his face, arms, and body were painted with mud that dries whitish-gray, exactly the color of a wolf's hair. Thrown over their shoulders and backs were wolf skins, with heads, pulled down over their eyes so that I could not see their faces by the fire that was in thick willows by a water-hole. I tried hard to know them, but could not guess their names.

"They knew I was puzzled and were pleased, often whining like real wolves in the shadows by the fire and acting as wolves do when they play. If they would only talk a little I thought I should know them, but when one said, 'Young man, go to the fire of Medicine-arrow and ask him for some fleshings for soup,' his voice did not help me. But I got up at once and went to Medicine-arrow's fire. 'Give me some fleshings for soup,' I said simply. [Fleshings are the thin shavings of meat and fat scraped from fresh buffalo hides in preparation for tanning.]

" 'I have no fleshings, young man,' said Medicine-arrow, putting dry willows on his fire before several other warriors who were smoking there. 'Go to that fire down yonder and ask Leads-the-wolf for fleshings. Perhaps he may have some,' he added.

"I went, willingly enough. I was very anxious to please everybody on the world just then. But Leads-the-wolf had no fleshings and directed me to another fire that sparkled among the willows. I visited it and other fires, even after I began to believe the Wolves were joking me. Nobody laughed, not that I saw, anyway. I think, however, they were laughing inside by the time I got back and told those Wolves who had sent me begging that there were no fleshings to be had.

"Those by the fire said nothing at all when I told them this. They did not even look at me, and because I did not know who they were I felt more foolish than ever. I made up my mind right there to wait until they slept and then somehow get a good look at their faces. But I was young and sleepy and, although I stayed awake until the Wolves spread their robes and lay down with their wolf skins so low over their eyes that I couldn't recognize them, I went fast asleep before they did.

"When I wakened, their robes were empty. They had gone about their business of the day without the least disturbance to me, and I did not see them again until night. Then they made a slave of me, and I carried water, roasted meat (eating only the poorest myself), caught up horses, and waited on everybody who called or bade me do anything, until we were all back in our village. But not once did a man in that party laugh at me, and not a person in the tribe who was not with us ever heard a word of the fun they made of me on that trip. This is the way of war-parties, as I have already said. Everything that happens is buried forever."

As I well knew that to be true, I was certain Plenty-coups had not told me half that might have been recounted. Long before now I had obtained more complete details of a young Indian's first venture on the war-path, and while I could have wished the Chief to be more open, I was obliged to be satisfied with what I had. He began to converse with Coyote-runs, and I realized he was trying to fix a date in his mind.

## VIII

"ANYWAY, it was summer," he said. "The War-clubs selected a site in the Bighorn valley and ordered the village set up in seven small circles, themselves making a great circle with the chief's lodges pitched in the center. This arrangement was a warning to us all that trouble was near, that our Wolves had seen something to be afraid of.

"That very day the Sioux attacked us, and we had a desperate fight with them, losing many warriors before we finally drove them back into the hills where they made a stand behind breast-works. It was night before we could dislodge them, and even then our victory cost us many lives, so that while we had really whipped the Sioux we felt that we ourselves had been beaten. The wailing of our women set the hearts of the young warriors afire, and they burned to avenge our dead.

"That night I learned that a war-party was forming to go into the Sioux country, and that Bell-rock, whom you know, was to carry the pipe. He is four years older than I am, and strong for his age. He was a brave warrior then and had many followers. Seeking him out, I joined his party. Any one of several other good men would have made a good leader. There were Bear-in-the-water, Fire-wind, Medicine-magpie, and Half-yellow-face, who later on became a scout with Son-of-the-morning-star [General Custer] on the Little Bighorn.

"We set out at daybreak, just when the village was beginning to move toward the mountains, and all day traveled southeast without seeing the enemy, or even many buffalo. When we camped for the night Bell-rock told us that next morning we would take to the high hills so that we might watch the game as we traveled toward the enemy's country. This started an argument between our leader and Yellow-tobacco, who insisted that we ought to go straight to Goose Creek. 'The enemy is there,' he said. 'I have dreamed, and in my sleep saw the enemy camped on Goose Creek with many, many horses. Six of them are for me.'

"Yellow-tobacco was a white man [George Reed Davis], a trapper who had taken a Crow woman and had lived with us a long time. I liked him. He was a member of the Foxes, like me. I thought Bell-rock ought to listen, but he would not, and so in the morning when we started for the high hills as commanded by our leader, Yellow-tobacco left us. 'If you will not go to Goose Creek where the enemy is camped, I am going back to my woman,' he said.

"His dream would have saved us a lot of traveling if we had listened, but you see Bell-rock had divided our party and agreed to meet the ones he had sent on different routes at a given place, so he was right in not agreeing with Yellow-tobacco. But that white man's dream was true. The enemy was camped on Goose Creek when we found him [where Sheridan, Wyoming, stands today].

"On Cloud Peak we met the other parties and soon picked up the enemy's trails, one coming in from the Black Hills, and one from the west. The *sign* was fresh and heavy, as though many lodges were somewhere ahead of us. Near sundown our Wolves brought us word that there was a large village on Goose Creek, exactly where the dream of Yellow-tobacco had shown it to be.

"And what a village it was! It reached from Goose Creek to Tongue River. Five drums were going at once, and the big flat was covered with horses. I could count more lodges than I had ever seen before at one time. We should stand no chance against such a village, but we could steal some horses. I looked at the sky. The moon was already there waiting for night, and there would be little darkness.

"Our leaders were holding a council. By and by they stood up, Bell-rock beckoning me, and Bear-in-the-water calling Covers-his-face. We both went to them to get our orders. We, with several others selected by Half-yellow-face and Fire-wind, were to go into the village and cut as many horses as we could while the rest of the party stood ready to cover our retreat when we should be discovered. My heart sang with pride.

"Covers-his-face and I stole together to the edge of the village and waited for darkness. But it did not come. Instead, the moon grew brighter and brighter. But as though to reassure us the five drums kept beating, telling us the enemy was dancing, and that he was too busy with his pleasure to watch his horses. Nights in summer are very short, the light would come soon, and we dared not wait too long. 'Let us go in,' I whispered finally, and we tied our horses. I hated to leave mine. He was the best I had ever owned, but of course I could not take him with me.

"Before I knew it Covers-his-face had disappeared. I was alone among the enemy lodges, and the nearest was a Striped-feathered-arrow! No wonder the village was so large. The Sioux were not alone. They had company, and this might make them stupid—sure that no enemy would dare attack them. So many lodges made me feel lonely, and I turned my course to where they were not so close together. My eyes could not look behind, ahead, and on both sides at once. I went away from the thickly pitched lodges until I reached a very tall one that stood a little apart. A fine bay horse was tied there. Immediately I set my heart on owning him. I saw I should have to be careful because the lodge-skin was raised from the ground. And next I made out that the lodge was an Arapahoe! The three worst enemies our people had were combined against us, with the intention, I believed, of making quick war on us. ["Arapahoe" in the Crow tongue means "Tattooed marks, plenty of."]

"But my eyes were on the bay horse most of the time now. He was eating grass before the Arapahoe lodge, and the rope around his neck reached into it. Somebody loved him and slept with his hand on the rope. I could not blame him. I thought the bay might be as good as the Deer, my own good war-horse tied at the edge of the village. No Sioux owned a better horse than he. It occurred to me more than once that they might steal him while I was stealing one of their horses.

"I crept a little closer. The lodge-skin was lifted in front, the rope going into the blackness inside. I tried to see under the lodge-skin, but the moonlight made a big, bright ring around it that stopped at the lodge-poles as though afraid to go farther. I could see nothing inside and there were no sounds. I would chance it! I was flat on the ground by the bay horse, my knife lifted to cut the rope, when somebody stirred, moved a bit inside the lodge. My hand with the knife came down to my side. The Arapahoe was awake and watching his horse!

"The shadow of the bay was on me, and I dared not move. I heard the five drums, one beating in the middle of the village and two at either end, far off. I must not stay there too long. Even if the Arapahoe did not see me, the other Crows might be discovered, and then I should be caught and killed.

"I crept out of the bay's shadow like a wolf until I had got his form between me and the eyes I felt sure were watching from the blackness of the Arapahoe lodge. Then I went swiftly until I came to another horse. He was a cream with white mane and tail, a good horse, but not so good as the bay. He was tied to a Sioux lodge that was dark and still. His owner was dancing, and while he enjoyed himself I cut his horse's rope. But I wanted the bay. I could not go away without him. I would have another try anyway.

"A cream-colored horse is difficult to see in the night, especially in the moonlight. I would make him help me steal the bay. Leading him, and yet crowding against his body to keep myself hidden from the sharp eyes in the Arapahoe lodge, I managed to reach the bay again, expecting to feel an arrow in my side or see the flash of a gun out of the black hole beneath the lifted lodge-skin. The horses, wondering what was going on, touched their noses together, their warm bodies pressing against my naked sides, while I stared into the black hole. Nothing stirred there. Perhaps the man had gone to sleep. I would find out.

"Instead of cutting the bay's rope I tied my own rope around his neck. Dropping the coil at his feet, I kept hold of the other end and slipped away, leading the cream till my rope was stretched. Then the cream and I stood still while I began slowly to pull on my rope. The bay, thinking somebody wanted him, began to come toward me, and as he came I kept coiling my rope, until he stopped short. He had reached the very end of the Arapahoe's rope, you see, and could come no farther. I was very careful now to look and listen. If the Arapahoe pulled in his rope, taking his bay back with it, I would let him have my rope that was tied to his horse's neck and go away from there with the cream. But he did not pull. The bay horse, wondering what somebody was trying to do with him, stood still with two ropes around his neck. The Arapahoe who owned him was asleep!

"I led the cream back to the bay and cut the other fellow's rope. I knew it was time I was away from there now, so I hurried with my two horses to the edge of the village where I had left the Deer. But before I was halfway a shot cracked, then another. I sprang upon the bay and, leading the cream, lashed them into a run, wondering what had become of Covers-his-face.

"The first Crow I met was Bell-rock. He was leading the Deer. When I raced up to him he tossed me the rope. 'Keep him,' I called. 'Somebody will need him.' The big village was aroused. Guns were cracking. There was no time now to stop and change horses, and I tossed the rope of the Deer back to Bell-rock. But he did not catch it. The Deer was left behind; my wonderful war-horse was mine no longer. The Sioux that got him was a lucky man.

"I thought that Covers-his-face had been discovered and had started the fight, but instead, those who stampeded the loose horses just outside the village brought on the fighting. I saw that we had a large number of horses, but did not wait to talk to anybody and raced away for the place where we had left our clothes with two men to watch them. It was on the right of Tongue River, just at the canyon. We called it The-place-where-the-cranes-rest. The bay horse was fast, and I reached the place first. 'Get ready!' I cried, springing from the bay and getting into my leggings and shirt, 'our party is coming.'

"I could hear the pounding hoofs, even when my shirt was over my head. Before my clothes were decently on me I had seen the pointers [men in the lead to guide the running horses] and close behind them many frightened horses. The enemy was after them too. Guns flashed as our men turned on their horses to shoot back in the gray light of breaking day. There were four Crows in the lead, and they were riding like the wind toward a steep-cut bank, a regular canyon! Did they not know it was there? It seemed to jump up before my eyes and to run to meet my friends. What would they do?

"Not knowing yet how I could help them I dashed for the river. I dared not call out or wave my arms to warn them, for fear I might turn the whole band and cause a stampede that would lose what we had gained. I stopped still, my breath nearly choking me, when the first horse went over the brink. They all went over—horses, riders, like a swirl of dry leaves in a gale of wind. And before I could take ten steps they were coming out —alive! I could not believe my eyes! Only one man was hurt. His face was smashed and his horse killed under him. I was happy again.

"We soon reached the timber where we had the best of it and drove the enemy back easily. Three days later we rode into our village singing of victory, and our chiefs, Sits-in-the-middle-of-the-land and Iron-bull, came out to meet us, singing Praise Songs. My heart rejoiced when I heard them speak my own name. The village was on Arrow Creek, near the Gap, and was getting ready to move. But Iron-bull stopped all preparation until he could give us hot coffee to drink. It was the first I had ever tasted, and I shall never forget it, or how happy I felt because I had counted my first coup.

"This is all of the story; but I left out something I ought to tell you. When we were in the timber where we drove back the enemy, Covers-his-face found that the animal he had stolen in the village was a mare. He felt disgusted and declared he would go back and steal a horse. We tried to talk him out of his plan, but he was determined. 'I will wait here for you,' said Bear-in-the-water, who had given his horse to the man whose face had been smashed, and so was himself afoot.

"'All right,' said Bear-rears-up, 'if Bear-in-the-water waits here I will wait with him.' So we left them to do as they pleased and for ten days heard nothing more of them. We had begun to believe they had been killed, when one day the three came in, each riding a good horse that Covers-his-face had stolen from the Sioux. He told us he had found the lodge of a young man who was so jealous of his wife that he camped far from the nearest lodges of his friends. He had three very good horses tied to his tepee, just one apiece for Covers-his-face and his two friends waiting in the timber. This is what a man gets for being so jealous of a woman that he cannot be sociable with other men."

The three old fellows laughed heartily over the theft of the horses from the jealous Sioux. And downstairs two women were chuckling, as though they too had heard and enjoyed the joke.

## IX

"TELLING these things stirs my mind," said Plenty-coups, happily. "Many happenings are crowding to be told, but I am thinking now of the show the Sioux made to get even with us for the raid against them on Goose Creek. The three tribes [Sioux, Cheyenne, and Arapahoe] came against us, but we had a good Helper that evened things for us this time. It was the high water in the big rivers. They were bank-full and running wild. If it had not been for the river's help we might have had a hard time saving ourselves.

"We were on the Bighorn when our Wolves discovered the enemy in our country. He had already seen our village. There was no good to be gained by silence, or by trying to hide. But the Bighorn with its banks level-full was between us, and neither of us could cross it without giving the other a great advantage. So we showed off to each other and had a great time. I cannot tell you how beautiful the enemy looked, dressed in bright colors and wearing wonderful war-bonnets of eagle-feathers that waved in the wind. Many rode pinto horses, and parties of young warriors would often dash toward the river as though they intended to swim it, giving their war-whoops and daring us to come over the water to fight them. As there was danger that they might attempt to cross, each time a band of Sioux rode to the river we raced down on our side to meet them, told them in signs what we thought of them, dared them to come over, and made great fun of them as warriors; but we had no thought of swimming the Bighorn in the face of such numbers. They were fine to look at, rushing in and out among the bushes that were loaded with reddening berries, the sunlight making their finery glisten; and out on the plains, where the wind played with the feathers on the bonnets, they were continually yelling and showing off as much for their own women as for us.

"At last they began to move downstream, and of course we followed on our side. We did not dare leave them to themselves for fear they might cross and attack us. It was better to keep them in sight, and we did, setting up our village on Two-leggings Creek, where now there is a bridge. The enemy moved to the Little Bighorn and pitched his lodges on the flat where Chief Crooked-arm lives today. We could hear his drums going all night long, and if he was listening he might have heard ours. How the sound of those enemy drums set my blood burning! I went out alone and asked the Little-people to permit me to distinguish myself and die *now,* instead of living to be old. But I saw no sign, got no word, and had to go back and listen again to the drums.

"Suddenly ours stopped beating, and there was silence. Lodges began to come down, and horses to be packed. We moved in the night, ran away from our enemies. My heart shamed me then, but now I understand that our chiefs were right. The enemy was too numerous, and if we had given him battle we might have been wiped out. But youth is like fire—marvelous, and yet dangerous without control. Even after we had camped on Fly Creek my heart was in revolt against our action. I told myself that I could not permit the enemy to go away without striking at him, and that I did not intend to.

"I secretly talked with two of my friends, Big-shoulder and White-faced-horse. Both agreed to go with me against the allied village on the Little Bighorn, if we could get out of camp without being seen. The War-clubs were watching all young men, and now that we had agreed to go against the enemy, we three let our consciences make us believe they were keeping their eyes especially on us. But one by one we managed to sneak out of the village and hide our war-horses in a wash-out quite a way below it. By the middle of the day we were all in the wash-out waiting for night, and the time till then seemed endless. Twice we saw members of the War-clubs looking for us and once we heard a man tell another that we three were hot-heads and would never come back.

"When night finally came we crawled out of our wash-out and rode away under the stars until we reached a water-hole on the plains. Here, with the mud that was plentiful around it, we made ourselves look like wolves, even painting our horses with the stuff so they too would be difficult to see. We often fooled the enemy in this way, and I suppose he as often fooled us. To-night we felt obliged to outwit not only a possible enemy but also the War-clubs, who would be searching for us.

"We had but one horse apiece, our best ones,

and to keep them fresh we walked and led them until we arrived at the junction of the Little Bighorn and Bighorn rivers. They were swollen and looked fat, like a buffalo cow. There seemed to be a raised streak in the middle of the stream and on it racing logs and roots of trees so thick I wondered if we could swim between them. It was cloudy and very still, but too light to cross; so we hid until dark came and then started.

"I was first to leave the shallow water, and in a flash of time I could not see my companions. The water took hold of me and my horse, whirling us along in the darkness with rocking logs and trees on all sides, till, after a hard fight, I felt the muddy bottom beneath my feet and stood up. My horse, glad to get his breath, stopped beside me, sinking down in the soft mud a little, while I listened for sounds of my companions. I knew I ought to hear their swimming horses. One can always do this, if one is near, but I could hear nothing except the humming of clouds of mosquitoes. Perhaps, I thought, the mosquitoes were stopping all sound from reaching me. My naked body was covered with them. I decided to move upstream, across from where I started, and learn why I was alone. I dragged in my little raft that held my shirt and leggings, and with my clothes and weapons under my arm made my way through the thick willows and alders to a place

I thought was directly across from the point where I had entered the river. There was no sound to be heard, and I could not see far through the clouds of mosquitoes that covered my body like a robe. 'What is the matter over there?' I called softly.

" 'White-faced-horse has hurt himself on a snag. You had better come back,' Big-shoulder answered.

"My little raft was far below me now and, as the bushes and mosquitoes forbade my going back after it, I quickly made another with some driftwood, to save my clothes and weapons from the water, and recrossed.

"We found a hole and kindled a small fire. In its light we saw that White-faced-horse was too badly cut to go to war. 'I will go back alone, and will start now so that you two may go on,' he said, after we had dressed the deep wound in his side. 'What shall I tell them in the village?' he asked.

" 'Tell my uncle, Chief White-horse, if I am not back in the village within four days he may begin to mourn for me, because I shall have gone home by the other trail,' I told him.

" 'Good!' he said, as we helped him mount his horse to ride away.

"Big-shoulder and I waited until nearly daybreak before we swam the river. We drifted even farther down than I had, but reached the shore in a better place, near some high hills which we climbed at once. Our robes were a little wet, and we spread them where the sun would dry them when he should come into the sky, thinking we should stay there until night. But scarcely had we settled ourselves when we heard shots, several of them, and not very far off. The day was not yet light enough to see to shoot. This puzzled us. We learned later that the Sioux had been told by white trappers about the Fourth of July. I had never heard of that day, and of course could not guess that the Sioux were celebrating it in the white man's fashion.

"I climbed a higher hill and with my glass saw a village moving from the west toward the east. Its head end was quite a distance from its rear, which was getting farther behind because of the slowness of its people. Some of the lodges at its lower end were not yet down, and they would have to hurry to catch up and close the line of moving travois which now had a long gap in it. Here was our opportunity.

"I ran back, and while dressing told Big-shoulder what I had seen. 'We will go out where we can watch them,' I said, 'and when the two ends are as far apart as they are likely to get we will ride between them and get among the scattered hunters who are sure to be out for meat.'

We acted quickly, but once we had ridden between the two ends of the moving village we knew we should soon be discovered; and we stopped behind some big rocks that stuck out of a hillside to look around us. We saw several Sioux hunters, scattered and far apart, as I expected. We rode no farther.

" 'Now we have our chance,' said Big-shoulder. 'You went into the Crazy Mountains and dreamed. Use your medicine today, and I will use mine.'

" 'Good,' I agreed, and laid my rifle on one of the rocks to undress for battle. The wind was blowing freshly when I stepped out from the sheltering rocks that it might strike my naked body. I spoke to my medicine, the stuffed skin of a Chickadee, which I held in my hand."

Plenty-coups showed intense feeling. He stood up, his moccasined feet spread wide to support his aged body, and addressed his open empty hand as though he were once more alone on that wind-swept hill. He was living his youth again. The chickadee was in his hand. He could see it there, and spoke to it as he had spoken that day so long ago when his medicine was his very life. The fanatical fervor in his half-whispered words thrilled me and made his own withered hand tremble.

"O Chickadee!" he said, "I saw the Four

Winds strike down the great forest. I saw only one tree, your tree, when they had finished. The Four Winds did not harm you, Chickadee. You told me to use the powers that Ah-badt-dadt-deah had given me, to listen as you did, and I should succeed. I have tried to follow your advice, shall always follow it. Help me now! The Four Winds are before me, the Four Winds who are the enemies of my people. Help me to strike them! Help me to count coup against them and to carry one of their scalps to my people whom I have promised to see again in two more days. As you stood alone in that great forest against the Four Winds, help me today to stand alone against my enemies."

He settled back into his chair, as though he had been carrying a burden and had suddenly been relieved of it. His thick chest was heaving, and I saw that his hand still shook when he accepted a lighted cigarette from Plain-bull.

"I tied the stuffed Chickadee beneath the left braid of my hair, just back of my ear," he went on, smoke from the cigarette coming from his lips with his softly spoken words. "It was so small that it could not be seen, even by Big-shoulder, whose medicine was the fantail of a blue grouse, with eagle breath-feathers. He tied his likewise beneath his braid, and I could see the breath-feathers blowing in the wind. Nothing can strike a breath-feather. It is light as air.

"Together we walked to our clothes and weapons, and while I put on my shirt and leggings, I said, 'The old men have told us that nothing here can last forever. They say that when men grow old and can no longer eat hard food, life is worth little. They tell us that everything we can see, except the earth and sky, changes a little even during a man's natural lifetime, and that when change comes to any created thing it must accept it, that it cannot fight, but must change. We do not know what may happen today, but let us act as though we were the Seven-stars [Big Dipper] in the sky that live forever. Go with me as far as you can, and I will go with you while there is breath in my body. Let us both remember there are two sights on our guns, and not shoot until we have seen them both. Let us shoot at a man's body where it sits on his horse, so that we shall not miss our marks altogether.'

"A deer ran past us, and looking down the hill I saw a warrior riding a gray horse. He had a gun and was a Sioux out hunting meat. While we looked he got off his horse and tied it to a small tree. I thought he must have seen us, so we drew back behind the rocks. But he had only seen a deer which he intended to kill, and he began walking slowly toward it, and us, too. I could count his steps, but he was out of range, and a wild shot would spoil our chance of success. We waited, watching his every movement, saw him raise his gun to shoot at the deer when his own head was behind a tree from us, saw that he had missed, heard his bullet whistle over our heads, watched him turn and start back for his horse. Ho! our time came, now. When the Sioux disappeared behind a little knoll we sprang on to our horses and dashed after him!

"My horse was faster than Big-shoulder's. The way was downhill, and I was nearly on the Sioux when he heard my horse's hoofs and turned his head. Ho! His steps down that hill were long now. Before I could reach him he had swung up, half on to his horse, struck him with his quirt, and was away, with me right behind him. I saw he was a fine man, and that he had spent the night in dancing. I knew this because his shoulders were painted red, his face yellow, with little lines of red over his eyes. I tried to draw a bead on him, but my horse was running fast, and I could not find my front sight. He looked back, saw me trying to shoot him, and began to throw his body from one side to the other on his horse. Not once did he try to use his own gun.

"Gaining on him, I at last managed to catch my front sight through the notch on the hind one, and pulled my trigger. My ball struck him in the right armpit, somehow cutting off three fingers from his left hand. He reeled in his saddle but did not fall, and I closed in on him. When I threw my arms around him to pull him from his horse, I saw blood in his nostrils and knew he was done for, though he held on to his saddle so tightly I could not pull him down. We were racing down the hill and must soon run into more Sioux. There was no time to lose. I pulled very hard, wishing I could reload my gun and still hold him.

" 'Lean over! Lean far over!' I heard Big-shoulder behind me. Instead of leaning over I pushed the Sioux away from me, just as the smoke from Big-shoulder's gun spurted between us. The Sioux went down, and I fell with him, clutching his gun tightly.

" 'Catch his horse!' I shouted to Big-shoulder, who was going so fast his horse had to jump over the Sioux and me, or fall.

"The Sioux was full of fight, even yet, giving me trouble for a little while. However I had much the better of it and finished him before Big-shoulder caught the horse. He had a fine scalp, the hair long and nicely braided, like the one I had seen on the sun. And his clothes were beautiful; his gun-scabbard was beaded and so were his leggings, but his gun was empty. The foolish man had not reloaded after shooting at the deer. I understood now why he had not tried to shoot me. Those old muzzle-loading guns were bad, after a first shot was fired. One might as well depend on a club as on an empty gun. We used to wait until an enemy had fired and then charge him before he could reload.

"Big-shoulder brought in the fellow's horse, a good gray; and there was a fine, black blanket on the saddle. As we had made a lot of noise, we felt it was time we were away from that place. We were in plain sight of several Sioux, and yet nobody saw us. My medicine was strong that day. It has always been strong.

"We rode down a long coulee, reaching the Little Bighorn without even being chased. We followed it downstream until we came to where the Bighorn joins it, crossing there, about where the city of Hardin stands today. The water was darker colored and there were more logs and trees in it than when we had crossed before. We waited for night, and when we could scarcely see led our horses into the stream. My horse was a strong swimmer, and, leading the gray Sioux, I swam beside him until I reached the middle of the river. Here Big-shoulder's horse gave up and began to drift without fighting to get across. When a horse quits like that he will nearly always drown. I must do something to help my friend. But what? I had all I could do to take care of myself.

"I spoke to the Little-people, my Helpers. 'Take this gray Sioux,' I said, 'and the scalp that hangs on his saddle. Help my friend.' I tossed the gray's rope over his back and let him go. He seemed to understand and turned downstream toward Big-shoulder, who caught him. They reached the shore far below, and when I saw them coming out of the angry water I thanked the Little-people with all my heart.

"Big-shoulder was singing as he came to me. 'Your gray Sioux saved my life,' he said. 'Your medicine sent him to me when I needed him. I should not now be alive if he had not come.'

"We both felt very happy there under the bright stars while we let our horses eat grass and rest before setting out again. We were young and loved life.

"At midnight a strange thing happened. We had stopped at a spring to drink and rest our horses. While I was lying near the water I noticed that the buffalo were moving restlessly on a flat toward the north. Without speaking of this to Big-shoulder I got up on my knees to look.

" 'Come here,' whispered Big-shoulder, from the willows.

"I crept near him, my gun ready. 'What is it?' I whispered, my eyes on the moving buffalo that were black spots in the night.

" 'Smell this!' he whispered, holding up my

Sioux scalp that was perfumed with beaver musk.

"I felt like slapping his face. I thought it a poor time to be making jokes; so, without smelling the scalp or even speaking, I crept out to the edge of the willows that were thick about the spring. Something that was not a buffalo was coming to the water!

"I leveled my gun at it. It might be a Crow warrior. 'I am going to shoot,' I said aloud.

"There was no answer, no sound except of Big-shoulder creeping nearer; the thing did not even stop at my spoken words. I stooped lower to get the thing between my eyes and the sky. It was a horse!

"I went out and caught him. On his back was a Sioux saddle and a Crow buffalo robe. Now we had four horses, two besides our old ones, and were nearly safe again. The Crow village was at the Hidden Tree, which white men call Ballantine.

"Long afterward, when I was a chief, I learned that the man I killed that day was a brother of Iron-cloud. I have forgotten the name of the man I scalped." (I think he did not wish to mention it.)

The odor of boiling meat had long ago told me that downstairs a meal was in preparation, and now the Chief's wife, clad exactly as she had been yesterday, came silently into the little room. She waited patiently until Plenty-coups finished speaking, then told him his dinner was ready and slipped silently down the stairs.

The Chief drew an open-faced gold watch from his pocket and held it before Braided-scalp-lock. "Where is the sun?" he asked, as though the hour made a great difference in his household affairs. But the timepiece had its uses, nevertheless. I had observed that whenever the old man began to grow tired he presented the watch to somebody's eyes, and if the hour was decently late, he quit talking for the day.

The rain had ceased, and although the grass and bushes were wet, I walked out to an apple tree I had seen the day before. It had been planted long ago and had flourished. I intended to ask if it ever bore fruit, but forgot to. The altitude of Pryor would seem to forbid apple growing, though there is wild fruit there. I ate my lunch beneath the apple tree, and then, because rain again threatened, walked to the barn and sheds to look around. I came first to the little log building that had once served as Plenty-coups' store. Its hewn logs had grown very gray and looked deserted. I should have liked to look about on the inside, but its door was locked and its windows boarded up. "Completely out of business," it seemed to say, "but when the Chief was merchant here there was much going on. His customers were in no hurry and told stories of war across my counters."

In the sheds were ancient mowing machines, rakes, buggies long out of date, wrecks of wagons, and an old self-binder on which at least a dozen chickens roosted at night. Most of the farming machinery was wretchedly battered and had been mended with baling wire, the boon of isolated mechanics. About the only goods I saw that were in condition were saddles. These hung safely upon the wheels of the farming machinery, and were regular stock saddles such as all cowmen use.

Aware that before the Chief would be ready to talk again he would consult the gold watch, I saw that I had yet half an hour to wait, so I walked out to the road, an abandoned railroad grade, the right of way for the railway having been purchased from the Crows through Plenty-coups.

Rain drove me back to the house, where I found the Chief ready to talk. His first words showed me he was growing anxious to go on with his story. "I have told you before that all the happenings which I recount will not always be in their proper places," he said. "At first I found it difficult to think of things to tell you, but now I think of too many. I have to hold them back."

## X

"THE Absarokees are red men," Plenty-coups began, "and so are their enemies, the Sioux, Cheyenne, and Arapahoe, three tribes of people, speaking three different languages, who always combined against us and who greatly outnumbered the Crows. When I was young they had better weapons too. But in spite of all this we have held our beautiful country to this day. War was always with us until the white man came; then because we were not against him he became our friend. Our lands are ours by treaty and not by chance gift. I have been told that I am the only living chief who signed a treaty with the United States.

"I was a chief when I was twenty-eight

[1875], and well remember that when white men found gold in the Black Hills the Sioux and Cheyenne made war on them. The Crows were wiser. We knew the white men were strong, without number in their own country, and that there was no good in fighting them; so that when other tribes wished us to fight them we refused. Our leading chiefs saw that to help the white men fight their enemies and ours would make them our friends. We had always fought the three tribes, Sioux, Cheyenne, and Arapahoe, anyway, and might as well do so now. The complete destruction of our old enemies would please us. Our decision was reached, not because we loved the white man who was already crowding other tribes into our country, or because we hated the Sioux, Cheyenne, and Arapahoe, but because we plainly saw that this course was the only one which might save our beautiful country for us. When I think back my heart sings because we acted as we did. It was the only way open to us.

"One day in the springtime [1876], when our village was on the Rosebud, the Limping Soldier [General Gibbon] came to talk to our chiefs about going to war with him against the Sioux, Cheyenne, and Arapahoe, who had been fighting his soldiers. We agreed, and when he asked us for some Wolves we gave him twenty men. These went away with him to his camp, where he told us he was waiting for The-other-one [General Terry] and Son-of-the-morning-star [General Custer].

"We moved next day, and when our village was at the mouth of Grapevine Creek, two other men came to see us. They had been sent by Three-stars [General Crook]. One was a half-blood Sioux, named Left-hand [probably Frank Gruard, supposed by the Crows to be half Sioux, but a native of the Sandwich Islands]. I do not remember the other's name or what he looked like. We met them in council. They told us that the Great White Chief [the President] had told Three-stars to ask us to help him. They said his camp was on Goose Creek [where Sheridan, Wyoming, stands now] and that he had many soldiers with him there.

"We listened until they had finished all they had come to say. Then I spoke: 'Let us help this man,' I said. 'His Wolves here say he has many soldiers in his camp and with them we shall whip our old enemies. Besides, we shall make the white man our friend. This is a fight for future peace, and I will carry the pipe for all who will go with me to the village of Three-stars.'

"One hundred and thirty-five young men offered themselves, and we got ready at once. Alligator-stands-up was our war-chief, and besides him there were many good men in our party. The Bighorn River was bank-full, but we were happy and before night were across it with camp made to kill buffalo for supplies. Two days after this we came to the hills that looked down on the flat on Goose Creek. I shall never forget what I saw there. It was nearly midday and countless little tents were in straight rows in the green grass and there were nearly as many little fires. Blue soldiers were everywhere. I could not count the wagons and horses and mules. They looked like the grass on the plains—beyond counting.

"The Wolves of Three-stars had seen us and had told him we were coming. Even before we dismounted to dress up and paint ourselves for war a bugle sang a war-song in the soldiers' village, after which many blue men began running about. Then, under our very eyes, and so quickly we could scarcely believe them, countless blue legs were walking together; fine horses in little bands that were all of one color were dancing to the songs of shining horns and drums. Oh, what a sight I saw there on Goose Creek that day in the sunlight! My heart sang with the shining horns of the blue soldiers in Three-stars' village.

"Our faces painted, we put on our war-bonnets and sprang upon our horses. We gave the Crow war-whoop, and, firing our guns in the air, dashed down the hill."

The old man grew excited. Rising, he gave the war-whoop, drumming his mouth with his open hand. His body was tense, his face working, his hands, signing his now rapidly spoken tale, were swift indeed. How he was riding! His old body swayed from side to side, and his imaginary quirt lashed his horse cruelly. I could fairly see him ride! I wish I might tell his story just as he did.

"Ho! Suddenly—like that—the soldiers stopped, the horses stopped, all in little bands!" panted the old Chief, sinking back into his chair exhausted. "All were in straight lines, *all,* with Three-stars and his head men on beautiful horses in the lead.

*"Whoooooooooo!"*

The urge was too great. The hour had returned, and the old man, standing again, gave the Crow yell so heartily that I dodged.

*"Whoooooo!* Our guns were cracking and we raised a big dust. We threw our bodies first one way and then another on our horses, just as we do when fighting. Some of us sprang to the ground and back again without even staggering our horses, and all the time our beautiful bonnets were blowing in the wind. Ah, that was a great day!"

He settled into his chair again, reaching for his pipe with trembling hands. "Three-stars was glad to see us," he went on, sobered by thoughts of what followed. "He put his right hand to his hat and held it there until we had passed him. Yes, and even until we had circled the whole village, riding very fast while all the soldiers stood still, their guns and the long knives of the horse-soldiers flashing in the sun's light. Then their guns spoke together many times—always together—and powder-smoke nearly hid their blue clothes. Oh, what a sight I saw that day on Goose Creek! My heart was afire!"

He fell silent and repeatedly brushed his face with his hand, as though wiping away thoughts of the summer of 1876. "When we camped near the village Left-hand, the Wolf who had visited us on Grapevine Creek, came to tell me and other chiefs that Three-stars wished to speak with us in his lodge," he went on, speaking very slowly. "I went at once, and Three-stars gave me his hand. 'I am glad you have come,' he told me. 'I have waited for you and Chief Washakie of the Shoshones. I am now three days late.' He led me to the shade of a tree. 'Sit down here,' he told me. 'I want you to know my chiefs.'

"He sent for them and I sent for mine, those who had not already arrived. We were glad to get acquainted before we got into trouble with our enemies; so there was much talking there in the shade of the tree, with Left-hand telling each what the other said. " 'We will wait here today,' said Three-stars. 'I am expecting a message from Elk River, and besides I expect Chief Washakie and his children this afternoon. We will give them a welcome, and I ask you to help me do this. As soon as Washakie comes we will start. I will wait no longer for the message. I am already three days late.'

"I noticed he had said these last words twice now, and I thought he was puzzled because the message had not come. While we were talking I heard the Shoshone war-whoop. Three-stars spoke to a chief near him and the chief went away from us. Quickly a bugle sang, and soldiers ran about, horses made dust, and out of it came the same beautiful sight we Crows had seen from the hills.

"I ran to our camp with the news, and instantly we mounted to help the soldiers welcome Washakie and his children. Guns cracked, horses ran, war-bonnets fanned in the wind, and the shining horns and drums of the soldiers sang for the Shoshones as they had for us. We joined our red brothers, who looked very handsome indeed, with their faces painted for war and their bonnets blowing about, like our own. Twice we rode round the village, and twice the guns of the soldiers spoke together, while our own were yelping like coyotes, no two together. Three-stars' heart was singing when he led Washakie and me to the shade, where he said over again the words he had spoken to me. His soldiers were laughing and giving presents to the Crows and Shoshones, who were dancing the war-dance to their own drums, many, many of them, beating as one. Our hearts were full, yet light as breath-feathers, while we looked at such numbers of fighting men—white and red—together. Never again shall I see such a sight.

" 'We can whip the Sioux, the Cheyenne, and the Arapahoe—whip anybody on the world,' I said to myself, as I looked at the countless men and guns and horses in Three-stars' village that day on Goose Creek. But I was wrong. Three-stars was whipped! And as Washakie and I were with him, we *all* got whipped good on the Rose-bud, as you shall see.

"Many of us had cartridge guns now, and the soldiers gave us whole boxes of cartridges, cans of powder, and more balls than we could carry. I had never before seen plenty of ammunition. My own people were always out of either powder or lead. We could make arrows for our bows, but we could not make powder or lead for our guns. But now everybody had more than he needed, more than he could use. And besides cartridges and powder, the soldiers gave us hard bread and bacon—too much of it. They had wagons filled with such things, and the soldiers were generous men. We had everything we wanted and we were in good condition to fight.

"I suppose Three-stars had his Wolves out on the hills. I know mine were out and had already seen the enemy. The country was alive with Sioux, Cheyenne, and Arapahoe. I told Three-stars about it, because I did not know his ways. He only said: 'We shall move in the morning. I hope to get a message from Elk River tonight.'

"I am certain no message came to him that night or any other time. None could have reached him. No messenger could have lived between us and Elk River. The enemy were like lice on a robe there, and hot for battle. That night when I was sleeping Left-hand came to me and said Three-stars wanted me. I rose and went to his lodge.

" 'Select nine good men and begin to scout at once toward the Rosebud,' he ordered me. 'I expect to meet The-other-one, the Limping Soldier, and Son-of-the-morning-star within two days,' he said. 'I wish you to lead your scouts yourself. We will follow you at daybreak and will march without resting from sun to sun,' he finished."

Plenty-coups asked for a cigarette, and Plain-bull lighted one, which the old man puffed with deep satisfaction. "I do not know why Three-stars believed he would meet those other soldier-chiefs within two days," he said, puzzled, "unless a message had reached him before we came to Goose Creek. He heard nothing from his friends after our arrival, I am certain. And if he had perfectly understood all that the Crow Wolves told him I am sure he would not have tried to go down the Rosebud at all. Crazy-horse was there, the Oglalla chief, with his warriors, on their way to join the big war-village on the Little Bighorn. Three-stars had been told all this many times and must have known the way was very bad, if Left-hand talked straight. Three-stars was a good man, and I have always believed that if he had understood all our Wolves told him through Left-hand he would not have tried to go down the Rosebud, but would have gone into the Little Bighorn Valley instead. I am always suspicious of interpreters. Too many have forked tongues."

I asked if Left-hand was Frank Gruard, but the Chief could not say. However, I believe Gruard was the interpreter, and if he was Left-hand there is no doubt about his ability or responsibility. "Anyway," said Plenty-coups, with a wave of his hand dismissing the matter, "it was the middle of the moon [June 16, 1876], and day would come before I reached the high hills. I hurried to pick my Wolves, nine of us, and leave the village. The stars were yet in the sky when we painted our bodies to look like wolves and climbed the hills. The great soldier village was still. Only a few men walked about with guns, while the rest slept in their little tents that were all in straight rows on the grass. A few fires were burning, and in their light stood white wagons, one behind another, until the lights of the little fires could reach no farther. The village of Three-stars was pretty to look at and made my heart sing. 'We can whip all the Sioux, all the Cheyenne, all the Arapahoe on the world,' I thought, wishing we might begin the fight at once.

"I scattered out my men and was soon alone. The stars were growing very dim by now, and while I was taking a last look at the soldier-village I heard a howl off to my right. I knew, of course, that it was a Sioux talking to his friends, and not a wolf that howled. He was telling his companions that he had seen the village of Three-stars, I believed. But anybody might see it. Nothing could be easier.

"I had told my Wolves to go slowly, to be careful, and to tell me any news they gathered; but since I had sent them out I had heard nothing from them. When day came I saw Sioux, several of them, and even made signs to them, which they answered. I felt good-natured toward them, because I thought we should soon give them a good whipping, and they were willing to joke with me a little, because they knew they had us in a very bad fix.

"The sun was beginning to warm the hills. I knew that by now the soldiers must be coming on their hard march. About this time I saw three buzzards in the air and stopped to watch them circling under the clear sky. I knew they saw something on the ground that was food for them, and I must learn what that thing was. Marking the spot that seemed to me to be the center of their circle, I went there as fast as I could. I found two fine horses. Both were dead, both were naked, without saddles or bridles; nothing was on them, except that *both had iron on their hoofs.* Now I had positive proof that Three-stars had received no messages from his friends on Elk River. I thought I had better tell him about the two dead horses which had belonged to soldiers; so I waited close by, watching the country, until Three-stars came along with his soldiers. [Crook had 1100 regulars, besides nearly 250 Indian allies, of whom all but 80 or 90 were Crows.]

"We camped that night, all of us, on the Rosebud. I thought it a bad place to choose when trouble was so near; and there was a worse place below, where Crazy-horse was waiting to trap us. Three-stars had left all his wagons on Goose Creek, packing his mules, and these were the last to reach our camp. The horse-soldiers came in first, next the walking-soldiers, and finally, when we were in our robes, the packers came. I had been out looking around before dark. I did not believe the night would pass without a fight; and I did not like our position. I told Three-stars we were near big trouble, hoping he would move to a better camp, but he did not.

"All night long the enemy gathered. Coyote yelps and Wolf howls in the hills told me he was closing in on us while I waited in my robe. I kept thinking about the bad canyon just below us and of our poor stand for a big fight, until I began to hear Owls; then I left my robe. I realized that Sioux, Cheyenne, and Arapahoe were thick about us, like ants on a freshly-killed buffalo's hide. We were going to have a hard fight in a very bad place.

"Before daybreak [3 o'clock] Three-stars was moving, with the Crows divided into parties ahead, and before the sun had been long in the sky we ran into the enemy. I fell back to be with Three-stars, for the big fight I knew was on our hands. He stopped when he heard the first shots, setting his men in position. This is the way I saw them: the pack-train was facing south, the walking-soldiers were among the bushes in the gulch, the horse-soldiers, afoot now, were facing east and north. There were two flags: one with the walking-soldiers and one with the horse-soldiers.

Everybody was ready for the trouble that was following us Crows as fast as it could.

"We swung in between Three-stars and the advancing enemy, facing west and a little north, with the Shoshones. Then, seeing that Three-stars was ready, we Indians charged the enemy, driving him back and breaking his line. But he divided and turned his ends around ours to get at Three-stars. When we saw this we turned back, with our wounded, because Three-stars needed us now. His horse-soldiers were backing up, leaving their position, when we got there; but his walking-soldiers in the willows were holding their ground. Sioux, Cheyenne, and Arapahoe were pressing them hard. I saw horse after horse go down and many a soldier go under, before the horse-soldiers began to run, so mixed up with Indians and plunging horses we dared not shoot that way. The enemy was clubbing the soldiers, striking them down, with but scattering shots speaking, when we charged.

"Our war-whoop, with the Shoshones', waked the Echo-people! We rode *through* them, over the body of one of Three-stars' chiefs who was shot through the face under his eyes, so that the flesh was pushed away from his broken bones. Our charge saved him from being finished and scalped."

The old Chief, clutching at his wrinkled face

to describe the officer's hideous wound, staggered against the wall, his husky voice trailing off into silence. I led him back to his chair, his face damp with perspiration. "We saved him," he murmured, accepting a pipe from Coyote-runs. "I do not know his name, or if he lived."

I was glad I knew the story of Crook's fight on the Rosebud. "He lived," I told him, "and the white man's history says that you saved him. His name was Guy V. Henry, a brave soldier and a good man. He was a little chief when you saved his life on the Rosebud, but grew to be a head chief before he died."

"I am glad, very glad," he whispered. "I can tell a brave warrior when I see him," he smiled, "and that man was brave.

"The enemy fell back," he continued. "He was fighting desperately, but losing, when suddenly I felt my horse break in two behind me. His front part staggered, slid a little way, and then fell. A bullet had broken his back. I struck the ground hard, and I rolled myself away from the many wild hoofs around my head, the Sioux yell in my ears. They thought they had me. I can hear them yet. They believed they were going to count coup on me, but I fooled them.

"Discovering a hole in a ledge of rim-rock, I worked my way there as fast as I could. Bullets slapped the stone, and dust flew up around the hole when I was going in. But I had kept my gun and did some good shooting from that hole in the rocks, until finally everybody got out of range. Then I crawled out to look for a horse to ride, and caught a fine bay with a black mane and tail.

"The Crows and Shoshones had now turned and were coming back, with the enemy pressing them very hard. I thought I had better try to reach the walking-soldiers, because I saw that we should all have to make a stand with them or lose the fight. But before I could get to them they began backing up. They were whipped and likely to run any time. While bullets were cutting the air around me, striking the ground, glancing to whine away, I made up my mind to ride for the walking-soldiers in the willows. I leaned low over my horse, lashing him to his best, till I felt him tremble like a leaf in the wind. Before I could even straighten myself on his back he went head first to the ground, dead. A bullet was in his heart. How the enemy did yell!

"I realized I was in a bad fix, but instantly I saw a gray horse with a saddle on his back. In less time than I am using to tell it I was in that saddle and away. The horse was no good. I had to beat him to make him even walk. Yet if he had not been so slow and lazy, I suppose I might have been killed. A Crow would not own such a horse as that Sioux gray.

"Just then I saw Alligator-stands-up, our war-chief, make the sign to form wings; so I turned with the nearest Crows. This was the end of the fight on the Rosebud. We Indians drove the enemy away down the creek."

Plenty-coups stopped to smoke, his face telling me his mind was busy with the events of that unfortunate day. I did not disturb him with questions, but myself reviewed my remembrances of the battle of the Rosebud, as set forth in our history. I found myself feeling astonished at the Chief's accuracy after so long a time. General Crook was whipped on the Rosebud, and the positions the troops occupied at the beginning of the battle were, I recalled, about as Plenty-coups had said. Waiving the old man's quite natural tendency to extol the importance of his people's part in the fight, his description of the day's action compares favorably with its written history. General Henry, then a captain, was shot exactly as described by Plenty-coups, and it is likewise true that if the Indians had not charged when they did he would have been killed and scalped. I was now certain there would be other historical details unfolded when the Chief should resume, and there were.

"The poor soldiers had suffered," he went on, laying the pipe on the floor. "They were whipped and wanted no more to do with Crazy-horse just then. I saw some strange sights that day. I met one soldier riding very fast with both his arms shot nearly off. They were hanging down like two strips of bloody meat.

"It was past midday when we began to help the soldiers pick up their wounded. I remember I wanted water, but though my tongue was like gravel on the dry ground in my mouth, I did not take the time to drink. There was too much to do for one to waste his time. We found many wounded soldiers in the bushes, and the dead horses I shall never forget. They were everywhere, often with wounded soldiers between them on the ground. I do not know how many men were killed or wounded, but there were a good many, and some of the wounded would die, I feared. We Crows had only one man killed, and he was not exactly a Crow. He was a Cree who had lived with us for years, so that we looked upon him as a Crow. Three Crows and three Shoshones had been wounded in the fight on the Rosebud, but when we charged the enemy at the beginning of the battle seven Crows had been wounded, making us ten disabled men, some of them badly shot. The Shoshones had been lucky. Not one had been killed. But there were more Crows in the fight to be shot at than there were Shoshones; so we had more chances to lose than they.

"I saw the soldiers do a foolish thing with that chief who had been shot in the face. The man was in bad shape, and to carry him away from the Rosebud they tied two poles between two mules and put the wounded chief on a blanket they had lashed to the poles. When the mules came to a steep hill the ropes broke and the mules ran away, pitching the suffering chief head-first down the hill. He did not complain at all. I liked that man. No Indian would have done such a thing with a badly wounded man. I should have liked to tell the soldiers how to handle their chief, but they did not ask me, so I had to keep still.

"I believe it was late that afternoon, though it may have been next morning, that Three-stars started back to his village on Goose Creek, where he had left some of his soldiers and all his wagons. We shook hands, and then we Crows went on to our own village with our wounded, ten in number. We had ten enemy scalps, a good many horses, saddles, and blankets. Of course, most of the enemy dead had been carried away by their friends so that we could not take their scalps. But we felt satisfied with what we had, and we still had plenty of ammunition for our guns, a thing we were always short of before we met those soldiers. We believed we had helped the white men and felt proud of it, but to this day the Government has paid us nothing for aiding Three-stars, who is probably dead now."

I felt glad of an interruption that came just here, although sorry the news brought was bad. An old warrior had passed away, and his son had come to tell the Chief. I wished to make a note that would remind me to look up the name of the man whose arms had been so badly torn by bullets. I remembered there had been such a man in the battle of the Rosebud. Later I found the written details. He was Bugler Snow, who had been sent out with dispatches by General Crook. The incident of General Henry having been thrown from the rude litter is also exactly true and may be read in the history of Crook's campaign.

There followed a short conversation between Coyote-runs, Plain-bull, and Plenty-coups, concerning the man who had just died. I began to be afraid the Chief would not continue telling his story, because of his respect for the dead man, which I knew was great. But he dismissed the messenger and resumed.

"The white men might have done a better job in their fights with our old enemies, the Sioux, Cheyenne, and Arapahoe, if they had been more careful and had kept together better. Son-of-the-morning-star was wiped out because he did not wait for his friends to help him do a big job."

"Why do you believe this? Who told you that

Son-of-the-morning-star should have waited for his friends before fighting?" I asked, to get his personal opinion of the bloody affair on the Little Bighorn.

"I have always believed it," he said, leaning toward me confidentially. "Nobody told me; nobody had to. Anybody would believe that way if he knew how things were around the Little Bighorn. I have always thought that The-other-one [General Terry] told Son-of-the-morning-star [Custer] to look a little for Three-stars, and that when he saw the enemy's trail he forgot, because he wished to fight. The-other-one must have known the country between him and Three-stars was alive with enemies. His Wolves must have told him this, since any Wolf would know it. I have never been told so, but I believe the two dead horses that had iron on their hoofs, the dead horses the buzzards showed me on the Rosebud, had belonged to two Wolves sent out by The-other-one to Three-stars, and that these chiefs expected to fight together against the village on the Little Bighorn."

General Terry's orders to General Custer are well known and have never ceased to excite argument. Even Terry's supposed oral order, in bidding Custer farewell, has been the theme of many articles exalting and condemning General Custer's actions on the Little Bighorn, June 25,

1876. I tried now to get the names of all the Crow scouts who went with Custer into the valley of the Little Bighorn, but I could not.

"Of all those Crows who fought with Three-stars, or went as Wolves with Son-of-the-morning-star, but fifteen are alive today," said Plenty-coups. "It is not good to speak their names, or I would tell them to you."

Then he changed the subject. "I lost two good horses with Three-stars on the Rosebud," he said, "and after the fight had trouble to keep any horses even here. The Sioux, Cheyenne, and Arapahoe needed horses very badly, and almost every night they came here to steal some of ours. We killed two of the thieves on Dog-head, but withal we had a good time while our enemies were having a heap of bad luck.

"I have forgotten the number of days after Three-stars fought on the Rosebud that the men who had gone away as Wolves with The-other-one and Son-of-the-morning-star came back to our village. We at first believed them Sioux, and a party of young warriors went out to meet them and give them battle. Quickly we saw that Half-yellow-face and White-swan were not with them, and asked about them.

"White-swan had been so badly wounded on the Little Bighorn that the white soldiers had taken him away on a steamboat, and Half-yellow-face, refusing to leave him, had gone too. When finally Half-yellow-face came back to us, I learned what he saw on the Little Bighorn. He had at first been with Son-of-the-morning-star but at last, when the soldiers divided, he had been sent away with another chief [Major Reno]. He told me that Hairy-moccasin, a Crow Wolf, had first discovered the big enemy village and told Son-of-the-morning-star, and that he, Half-yellow-face, had then tried to stop Son-of-the-morning-star from attacking it. He said that when the soldier-chief gave the order that divided his men, he had spoken to him, through an interpreter, saying, 'Do not divide your men. There are too many of the enemy for us, even if we all stay together. If you must fight, keep us all together.' He said Son-of-the-morning-star had not liked those words and that he had replied, 'You do the scouting, and I will attend to the fighting.'

"As soon as the soldiers had begun to separate into bands, as they had been ordered, Half-yellow-face had stripped and painted his face. 'Why are you doing all this?' Son-of-the-morning-star had asked. 'Because you and I are going home today, and by a trail that is strange to us both,' Half-yellow-face had answered. It was then that Son-of-the-morning-star sent Half-yellow-face with that other chief [Reno].

"He would have been killed if he had not been sent with that other chief, but as it was he and the others had a very hard time. It was Half-yellow-face and White-swan who led many of that other chief's men into a safe place among the bushes. And it was they who, when at last night came, showed these soldiers where they could creep away and cross the Little Bighorn to reach the chief who was on the hills with the rest of his men. Half-yellow-face and White-swan, who was badly shot, stayed in those bushes with the wounded white soldiers until The-other-one came and relieved them all, two days after Son-of-the-morning-star had been wiped out.

"It was now that we learned Son-of-the-morning-star had gone to his Father, and that all his horse-soldiers had gone with him. He had died fighting, as a warrior should, and there were two mortal wounds in his body. He had been foolish to attack so great a village alone, but he had been too brave to take his own life, like a coward.

"We knew even at this time that Curley, who had been with Son-of-the-morning-star, had got away from the soldiers before the fighting started on the Little Bighorn, and that he had gone back to the battle-ground with The-other-one. The white soldiers had been unlucky, but just the same they had broken the backs of our worst enemies. And we believed we had helped them do it. We could now sleep without expecting to be routed out to fight very early, and this was the first time I had ever known such a condition. I am tired. Will you come again in the morning?"

The watch was presented to Braided-scalp-lock, who said it was five o'clock; and I therefore left for my quarters, thinking particularly of the short and significant conversation between General Custer and Half-yellow-face, which the old Chief had repeated.

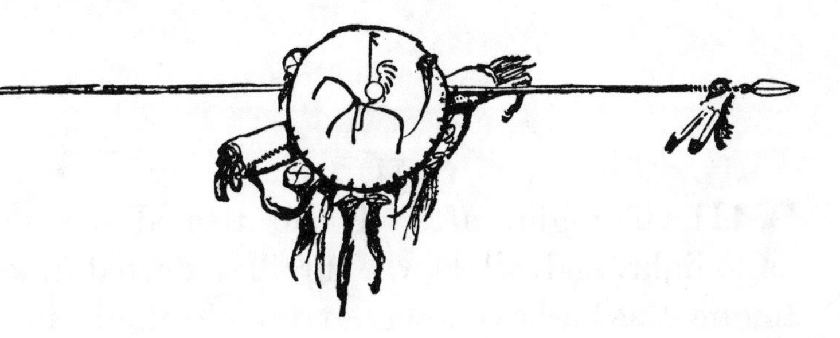

## XI

THAT night, after I had turned out my light and while the fireflies darted thick among the bushes along Arrow Creek, I could still see the sorrow in the old Chief's face as he told of the death of Custer. I recalled that Lieutenant James Bradley, who was with General Terry when the latter's command went to the rescue of Reno's men, had said in his priceless journal of the Custer campaign that "outside the relatives and personal friends of the fallen, there were none in this whole horrified nation of forty millions of people to whom the tidings brought more grief than to the Crows." "When they heard the story," says Bradley, "they one by one broke off from the group of listeners and going aside a little distance sat down alone, weeping and chanting that dreadful Mourning Song, and rocking their bodies to and fro."

I am familiar with the battle ground on the Little Bighorn. Its monument and scattered headstones tell an awesome story which tonight kept milling in my mind. I remembered thankfully that the terrible fighting must have ended quickly. In 1887 an old Cheyenne who had taken part in the annihilation of Custer's command had told me that the sun traveled only the "width of a lodge-pole" (perhaps twenty minutes) while it lasted. He had engaged to tell me the story of the fight. I had patiently waited while he peeled scores of little sticks with his thumb-nail and set them on a little mound he had raised between us, often changing their position and regrouping them to suit his memory. These little sticks represented Custer's men on the fatal hill, and I had hoped to gather something entirely new from this warrior who had been in the battle. But when at last his little sticks were in proper positions, he suddenly and very violently scooped them all between his hands and threw them spitefully away. "Pooof!" he said, blowing upon his empty palms. And this was all the story the old Cheyenne told me after so much preparation.

"Do you remember exactly how old you were

when Son-of-the-morning-star was wiped out?" I asked, after the usual greeting with Plenty-coups next morning.

"Yes," he replied. "I was twenty-nine when I fought with Three-stars on the Rosebud. I was a chief and had been married since I was twenty-four. My woman's name was Knows-her-mother. She was the daughter of Warm-robe, a man who once stood off a party of Sioux with only his bow and arrows. He had a gun, a flint-lock, fired it once, then threw it away, and fought off a large band of Sioux with his bow and arrows. His woman's name I dare not mention. She was my mother-in-law.

"Now I want to go back a little way to a winter before I fought with Three-stars. Word reached us that our brothers, the River Crows, were being pushed south of Bear River [Milk River] by the Crees, Yanktonese Sioux, Assiniboine, and some Blackfeet. These Crows had already been driven across the Missouri and had been joined there by the Hairy-noses [Prairie Gros Ventres], who were helping them fight, when we heard about the trouble.

"Sixty of our young warriors under Bell-rock, who carried the pipe, left our village to help them. The weather was extremely cold, and clear. When we reached the Missouri slush-ice was running as thick as it could live in the river, and the banks were so dangerous to our horses that we were obliged to chip away the sharp ice with our knives, so that it might not wound them in reaching the water. After swimming, we headed straight for Two Buttes [Little Rockies], where by scouting we hoped to locate the enemy.

"I carried the pipe for our Wolves and at day-break, with my nine men, set out from our camp on the south side of the mountains. We climbed the buttes and from their tops saw Bear River and all the wide plains covered with snow. A cold wind was blowing and there, on top of the buttes, dry snow whirled about us like dust on a summer day. The river, far off, was marked by two streaks of naked trees that bent in the sharp wind, and in a bend it made I could see the enemy's village, partly hidden by the trees. Closer to the mountains where we were, between us and the enemy, several small bands of buffalo stood humped up with their hairy heads to the cold wind. I had never seen a colder looking country. And somehow I knew there must be another village near. I began to use my telescope and, sure enough, in a little time found a second village, larger than the other and nearly two days' travel from it. Both were Sioux. We had seen enough.

"I went back to our camp with my men, howling like a wolf and kicking a buffalo-chip ahead of me to show our friends we had located the enemy. Everybody was glad, and we held a council to talk things over while we passed the pipe. I said: 'In the morning let us leave all our things here in this camp and go among the pine trees on the other side of the mountains. The trees are plentiful there, so we can hide among them with our horses until the enemy comes to kill some buffalo. There are several bands of cows and bulls close to the mountains on the other side, and between the hills and the upper village. The Sioux will need meat and are sure to come. When they do, we will strike them hard.'

"Bell-rock and the rest thought it a good plan, and we followed it. But we got fooled. No hunters came after the buffalo. We waited there in the snow three days and nights without seeing an enemy, or anybody else. It was a cold business, waiting there, scarcely moving for three days and nights without a fire. I was glad when Bell-rock said, 'Let us go back and get warm. Those fellows must have too much meat.'

"Two villages so close together offered a bigger job than we wanted, and, now that my plan had failed, our prospects were not very bright. The cold made every Sioux warrior who had meat enough stay by his fire, and this kept the villages full of men who would otherwise be out on the plains. But we thought we might steal some horses anyway, and the next morning Bull-that-does-not-fall-down, Big-shoulder, Bull-tongue, and I left camp for the upper village, intending to try.

"The upper village we found moving slowly down toward the other one. This pleased us, because it seemed to offer us a chance; so we hurried back to get the whole party to come up. But when we were all on the spot where we Wolves had seen the moving village, we realized that its lodges were being set up nearer the buffalo, and that it was going no farther. This pleased us even more. We hid in a little coulee to wait for darkness, the cold wind biting us meanwhile and making our horses shiver. At dark we began slipping in toward the lodges that looked so comfortable on the white plains.

"When we were as close as we dared go in a body, Bell-rock called me to go in and cut horses. I felt very proud of this distinction, listening to hear who else our chiefs would choose for this dangerous mission. One's companions in adventure mean a good deal. When Spotted-horse called Shows-a-fish I was surprised to hear him decline the honor. His forefathers gave us our Crow war-bonnets, which are distinctive, with their feathers reaching down the back from the headdress itself. This tail on the bonnet represents the backbone of a buffalo, and was given to our people by a dream that came to a grandfather of Shows-a-fish. But that night his medicine was bad, and he did not wish to go into the enemy's village. He was wise to refuse when he was called.

"The other selections—two of them—pleased me. Bear-in-the-water called Bull-that-does-not-fall-down, and Hillside called Bull-tongue. There was no time wasted. I asked Big-shoulder to hold my horse while I was gone, but Spotted-horse said, 'No, you married my sister. To hold your horse is my right.' As it *was* his right I handed him my rope, to go with the two others into the village, where I had only bad luck from the start.

"As was usual when selected men were sent into a village to cut horses, a detail was appointed to go into the pony bands and stampede as many of the animals as possible. This custom sometimes made trouble for the ones sent into the village itself to cut the best war-horses. It always made them hurry and sometimes got them caught and killed, because stampeders generally make more noise than men who are sneaking among lodges filled with enemies, looking for fine horses to steal. A stampede usually started a fight, too, and we three hoped tonight to get safely out of the village with a good war-horse apiece before the stampeders should commence their work.

"The night being dark, the bright fires in the lodges marked them plainly on the white snow. In the first one we passed I could see women and children playing a game by the fire. The children were laughing, and the women too. Of course we passed them by, and presently arrived at a lodge where a good horse was tied, a buckskin full of life. I was about to cut his rope and be satisfied with him, when a man wearing a white-blanket capote [hooded cloak] stepped out of the lodge door, looked right into my face, and then ducked back inside. We moved away quickly, expecting an alarm, but none came. I never understood why the man ducked back so suddenly.

"No stir was made. Not even a dog yelped. So we three began again to look for war-horses, or better, a chance to kill a Sioux and take his scalp. At last I saw a young man's head against a lodge-skin. It made a fine mark, and I cocked my gun; but my companions whispered objections. 'You cannot get his scalp, and we shall have nothing to show for our trouble,' they said.

" 'But I would rather have a Sioux's life than his horse,' I argued.

"We had passed two chances to take horses already, and I was beginning to wish I had cut a large pinto I had seen a while back. He was a good horse with eagle feathers in his mane and tail, but I passed him, hoping to pay the Sioux a better score. 'We must be doing whatever we intend,' I said, thinking of the stampeders, who would not wait much longer.

" 'Look there!' Bull-tongue was pointing to a lodge near us.

"I could make out many forms through the lodge-skin by the bright fire within. Young men were sitting close together and smoking. I could see the pipe passing from one to another. Each wore a buffalo robe tucked about his hips, and the upper part of his body was naked. A bullet below the ribs of one might easily go through another, perhaps more, if no bone was struck. By stooping low, I thought, one of us on each side of the door, we might kill several of those young men with two shots and still get away. I had squatted down, my gun cocked and ready, to see how my plan looked along my gun-barrel, when a footstep creaked in the dry snow behind me.

"A man—and he was a big fellow—was bending over me and looking into my eyes. I saw several things quickly. I saw the man was armed with a gun, saw my two companions slip away, and saw a lighted lodge just back of the big fellow and me. So I sprang between its open door and him!

"Not daring to shoot into his lodge he rushed

at me with his knife. I shot him, and he fell against my knees, knocking me back against the lodge, which shook and trembled as though it would fall. Somebody—a woman, I think—raised the lodge door, and the man's head fell inside with my fingers in his hair. And that was all I got, a handful of his hair.

"I realized I must get away. The Sioux war-whoop had sounded. My shot had started things moving, so I must be moving myself. The young men who had been smoking came pouring out from their lodge, some of them running through the fire to get out. I knew they did this by the cloud of red sparks that flew up through the smoke-hole. But I did not wait around there to see very much. I ran, trying to load my empty gun, spilling a good deal of powder and losing a ball before I made out to charge the weapon again.

"Fighting had now started between our party and the Sioux warriors. Crow bullets were tearing the lodges, and I heard women and horses squealing all through the village, as I ran toward my friends. We never learned how much damage we did them, but the next day they moved out of the country, which was the thing we wished them to do. My companions were safe, and we had but two men wounded, none killed, so that we felt satisfied to return home."

It seemed to me the Chief had forgotten his brethren, the River Crows, whose cause had engaged him to go to Milk River in the bitter weather. They were truly brethren, as he had called them, having detached themselves from the main tribe between 1840 and 1850 and, led by Chief Rotten-belly who had quarreled with his rival, Long-hair, established themselves in the Judith and Musselshell countries. This division of the Crow tribe, with one that had occurred much earlier, furnishes a hint as to how there came to be so many Indian tribes in North America, since it has already resulted in many differences in both customs and language. I believe the Crows came out of the far south, probably out of Old Mexico. In their legends, which I have compiled, are many references to sea monsters. "Did you see the River Crows and their friends, the Hairy-noses, while you were gone?" I asked.

"No. We were not looking for them," Plenty-coups said. "We were out to help them, not to visit with them."

## XII

"NOW I want to tell you about a time when my heart tried to jump out of my mouth," Plenty-coups said, folding a blanket to soften his chair's seat. "It was a year after the story I have just told you, only it was summer time. Our village was on the Stillwater. Berries were red, and rivers were fat. Covers-his-face, Lion-that-shows, Walks, and I had decided to go on a raid against the Sioux to pay them for killing two Crows.

"It was hard to get out of our villages to go on raids. The War-clubs watched us very closely, and there was good reason for their watching, because when young men are permitted to go off to war by themselves they not only get into trouble, but leave the village weakened. Once, before my time, when many young men had left our village the Sioux came and attacked it, nearly wiping us out. We have never been so strong since that terrible day.

"But we four thought our village could get along without us for a little time. We knew it was going to move, and we went along with it as usual, until it reached The-place-where-the-colts-died [Tulloch Creek], where we managed to fool the War-clubs and get away unnoticed. Next day we swam Elk River not far from the site of the present city of Forsyth. The water was swift, but we were young and made fun of the job. We always swam on the lower side of our horses, the rope-hand [next to the horse] over the animal's shoulder, and the other in the water helping the horse along. We killed a fat buffalo cow on the Porcupine, and camped to dry the meat a little over a fire, so that it would be lighter to pack.

"When we struck the breaks of the Musselshell we climbed a bluff to look for signs of the Sioux. Down on the plains buffalo were in motion. Cows were looking for their calves, and calves were looking for their mothers; so we knew there had been a hunt only a short time since. But no Sioux were in sight—no village anywhere that my telescope could find. Our enemies must have traveled fast to have disappeared so completely in so short a time. My glass settled finally on a spot that seemed raised, on a bluff far off. It was an eagle, and farther on, perched on another bluff, I could see another, and still another, like Sioux Wolves watching the country. They looked to me to be satisfied to sit where they were forever. This told me that there were no enemies near us.

"I was carrying the pipe and was determined now to travel on toward the east in the open day, letting the eagles do my scouting. 'Watch the eagles,' I told my companions. 'They will fly as we approach them, and as long as they light on the next butte to the east of them we need fear nothing. But if one of them circles and turns back, we will hide and send out a Wolf.'

"My plan worked beautifully, and near sundown we came to a newly deserted camp where many lodges had stood, but did not stop because our eagles were still willing to fly and light in the direction we wished to travel. But the next day, about the middle, the eagles turned back, circling high over us; so that now I knew it was time to send out a Wolf.

"I did send out a Wolf, and he had no trouble in locating the enemy. From a high butte we saw the Big River, fat and very strong, and across it, toward the north, the Sioux village, its lodges pitched in nine circles, themselves forming a great circle near the river. All this was beautiful to see, and we sat there on the bluff looking as though we could not take our eyes away. Just below the village I could see the tops of other lodges, which informed me that a second village was there, with not much country between; but I could not count the lodges. Trees hid most of them. It was all fine to look upon, with men and women passing between the two villages as though visiting, and the plain across the river dotted with more horses than we could count. And horses were what we wanted this time.

"Until the sun went down we watched, and even till the dusk was closing in, never tiring of what we saw. Then we went down to the river, stripped, hid our clothing and our guns, and waited a little for night to come nearer before we should cross. We knew we were apt to be in a big hurry when we returned, if we ever did; so we carefully marked the place where we were to enter the water.

"The way to the other bank was far and the landing we hoped to make, good; but there was something about the water just where we were that I could not understand. It was too quiet. It was as though it did not belong to the rest of the river. When I dropped an offering of fat buffalo meat into it, it sank like a stone. This was not right. Fat meat should not sink. I did not like the way the water looked either. Thinking it best to keep these thoughts to myself, however, I said nothing to my companions, did not even speak of the strangeness of the water, when together we started for the black line of the other shore.

"There was no wind, no swish of water, no sound except the snorting of our swimming horses. We were in the middle of the river, and the moon was coming into the sky, when Covers-his-face called out, 'Something is holding me!'

"I thought at once of the strangeness of the water, of the sinking back-fat, and my heart tried to jump out of my mouth. The moonlight fell full upon Covers-his-face, like a streak of fire-light from a lodge door. His horse was lifted out of the water! He was standing still in the middle of the Big River, where the bottom was far beneath him!

"I wanted to get away from there, but I turned my horse in his direction, my heart beating like a war-drum. 'What is it?' I asked, and I am sure my voice must have trembled a little.

" 'I do not know,' he answered. 'Something is holding me here. I cannot get my horse away from this place.'

"My own horse came alongside of his, and sticking out my foot, I kicked under him. My toes touched something that felt like greasy feathers, something soft and slippery. Wooof!

"When a man knows what he is fighting, his heart is strong. I could see nothing at all here. So when my own horse began to rise, to be lifted like my companion's, my heart tried to jump out of my mouth. But I swallowed it and put my hand on Covers-his-face. 'Are you hurt?' I whispered.

" 'No,' he answered, 'but I cannot get away from here. Something I cannot see is holding me. You had better get away, if you can.'

"Then whatever it was that held us let go. Both my horse and that of Covers-his-face began to sink down in the water. There was no sound, no trembling, nothing to let us know what was beneath us. Presently our horses began to swim again, as though nothing had happened."

The old man paused here to take a pipe from Plain-bull, his face as much of a mystery as his story.

"I never knew what lifted us out of the water in the Big River that night," he said solemnly. "I am not now trying to tell you, but it must have been some powerful Water-person who lived just there in the Big River. There are many things which we do not understand, things that are beyond us, and when we meet them in this life all we can do is to recognize their existence and let them alone. They possess rights here, given to them by Ah-badt-dadt-deah, just as we do.

"We came out of the water on the north bank, just where a big trail touched the river. It led through a cottonwood grove to the open plains, and was straight. I noticed a cottonwood snag that had no bark on it. It looked white in the moonlight, and there was evidence that some Sioux had once kindled a fire near it. I took one of the black sticks from the old fire-ring and marked the snag. It would show us exactly where to swim the river in a hurry and help us to keep a little below that bad place.

"Luck came to us now. The bright moon was going under a black cloud in the sky. It looked like a shining war-shield, very handsome, but I was glad when it hid away. We were between the two villages, as we had planned, and intended to wait for people visiting between them. Excepting our knives we had no weapons. These make no sound, and I believed we might take a scalp or two, besides stealing some horses, if the moon kept hidden away.

"But nobody passed. Everybody was through visiting for the night, and we knew there was a big dance going on in the upper village, by the drums that were beating. If we were going to accomplish anything it was time to try. The big moon was out again by now, too bright to permit us to slip among the lodges unseen. I asked my medicine for clouds and rain, and both came soon after. Now we could at least steal a good buffalo-horse apiece and get away.

"At the upper end of the village upstream we found a lodge that had twenty horses tied near it. Neither Walks nor Lion-that-shows had ever cut a horse, and now I wished to give them a chance to count coup. As the lodge appeared to be deserted I believed its owner must be dancing; so I did not wait, but, keeping Covers-his-face beside me, sent Walks and Lion-that-shows to pick a horse apiece from among the twenty.

"The sky was dark, and a little fine rain was falling. Everything seemed to be in our favor; but before the two had had time to reach the horses I discovered somebody, a man, moving about among them. I could see his head and shoulders over the horses' backs, and wondered if my friends saw him too, but dared not call out to warn them. I pinched the arm of Covers-his-face, and to show me that he saw what I did he pinched me. Suddenly, as though we had agreed to do it, we both rose from our creeping position, and, kneeling, saw *three* men among the horses!

"We were but four against whatever number might come against us, and yet we two could not run away and leave our companions. I put my hand on the shoulder of Covers-his-face, and we both settled back to wait. That was all there was to do—wait to learn what was wrong over by that lodge. But I could not stand the waiting. 'I will go over there,' I whispered. 'You stay where you are till I come back, if you can.'

"Down on my hands and knees, the level line of the horses' backs was against the sky; and even though the sky was covered by clouds there was light enough to show that nobody was now among the horses. The three men had gone! I stopped, looking carefully along the backs of the horses, more puzzled than ever. Ought I to go on over there or turn back to Covers-his-face? 'Go on, and have done with this thing,' my medicine told me. But I did not have to go far. My two men were creeping toward me.

" 'There is a man with those horses,' whispered Lion-that-shows. 'He saw us, nearly touched us, but dodged out of sight without even speaking. We think he went into the lodge.'

" 'This is a queer night,' I said. 'Wait back there with Covers-his-face, and if trouble starts bring my horse to the crossing place. I am going to try to find out who it is that was among the horses!'

"Whoever it was, he was gone when I got to the horses, and there wasn't a sound about the lodge. But just the same I felt like looking around before doing anything. The fellow might be hidden close by and with helpers who might take us all. I slipped to the next nearest lodge. It was dark and still, like the other. The dance had left nobody at home in that part of the village, and if only I could have got the man who had been among the horses out of my mind, I could have been happy. I'd look a little farther for him, and then go back and cut a horse from among the twenty, I decided, walking cautiously around the lodge. Back of it I found a horse and looked him over. He was black as night, and very fine—so fine that I could not leave him there. So, after putting a war-bridle on his lower jaw, I cut his rope. I led him back toward the twenty, thinking I would cut another from among them, but when I drew near I saw three heads above their backs. They did not frighten me this time. I knew they were my three companions, who had not done as I told them. 'This is a queer night,' I was thinking again, when a shot rang out in the lower village.

"We had not been near it and could not understand the shooting. Nevertheless the time had come for us to be moving, and we got out of there with what we had. I was riding my new black and leading a good mare that had a colt following her. Covers-his-face had my war-horse, besides his own, and a fine bay. The others had also cut a horse apiece from the twenty, so that we had done pretty well.

"Nothing bothered us in the river. There was too much behind us for us even to think of the thing that had held Covers-his-face in the water, and we grabbed up our clothes and weapons, almost on the run. Our pace was a little hard on the colt, but he was old enough to take care of himself if he could not keep up, and anyway we had to get out of that country. But when we stopped to hide at daybreak the colt was with us, as strong as any horse in the lot. Afterward he was with me on many a raid, and until a Sioux bullet ended his life I never let him out of my sight.

"When we reached the Big Muddy I saw something that made me stop very quickly. It was far off, but I knew it was a man's head sticking up over a knoll. We got our horses into a buffalo wallow and stripped ourselves for a fight, and none too soon. Twenty men were coming at us.

"But they proved to be Crows, and, instead of fighting, we were soon laughing and passing the pipe. Long-otter, a friend of mine, was out with a party going against the Sioux; so before I slept I told him how to get into the Sioux village, and about the man who had acted so queerly among the horses there.

"Next morning Long-otter's party went on toward the Sioux, while we, with two of his men who wished to return to the Crow village, started for home. There were six of us now, and we felt safer but watched the buffalo for signs of the enemy who might be after us. We were well down the Big Muddy when I heard a shot and stopped my party to climb a knoll and see what was going on. We had been seen by a large party of warriors, who were now riding toward us as fast as their horses could run. My glass told me that they too were Crows, and I ran toward them making the Crow sign [moving the arms like the wings of a large bird].

"Fire-bear carried their pipe. They had been in the lower Sioux village, we learned, while we had been working in the one upstream. It had been their party who had started the shooting there, and it was Fire-bear himself who had been among the twenty horses in the upper village. He had gone there alone, but seeing Walks and Lion-that-shows among the horses he was looking over, he had slipped away, believing them Sioux, and had joined his party in the lower village. We had driven him away, you see. We had a good laugh over that night's mistakes. It was the craziest night I had ever seen. Just the same, Fire-bear had been very lucky. He had cut eight horses and might have taken more, if a Sioux had not come out of a lodge and shot at him.

"We danced and sang now, because we felt

strong. Both our parties were going back to the Crow village, and both had done rather well, too. We joked each other about the 'man' who had been among the Sioux horses and pushed the jokes pretty far, feeling very happy over the whole affair, till I made a mistake.

"Fire-bear's face was not handsome at any time, but now it was the homeliest I ever saw. His lips were so badly swollen and cracked by the sun's heat that they resembled thick pieces of raw buffalo-meat. I began to laugh at his face, to make fun of his lips. 'What a pity your face is not on a Sioux, so that I might slap it with my quirt,' I said, while everybody laughed, except Fire-bear.

" 'You talk big,' he growled, and I saw that he was very angry. I had not meant to hurt his feelings. He was a big fellow of about my own age, and powerful as a buffalo-bull. I ought to have known better than to say any more. But somehow I let my fun get the best of my judgment, and said, 'No woman will ever kiss you, Fire-bear. You are unkissable!'

"We were both near the water of the Big Muddy, eating some meat. He sprang upon me, and I fell flat on my back. Before I could roll him over he had kissed me twice—booof! I got away from him and jumped into the water, washing my face with it and with sand, not only to rid my lips of Fire-bear's kisses, but to joke him further. He never knew it, but his kisses made me a little sick, and for a long time afterward thoughts of his kisses made me wish to scrub my lips with sand.

"We were two days swimming Elk River. Two of our Sioux horses would not swim until we finally tied willows along their necks so they could neither look back nor turn around. After that when we dragged them into the water they were obliged to swim or drown, and made it across like the others. We struck our village at the mouth of Rosebud and rode in singing, feeling proud of our accomplishments. Good and bad luck always mixed themselves on these raids," said Plenty-coups, his voice scarcely audible, "but of all the raids I ever was on this was the craziest; and yet nobody was hurt."

A young Crow, of perhaps twenty-five years, had listened to most of this story, sitting on the springs of the iron bed. His black hair, exceptionally long and glossy, was carefully braided and had lately been "banged" above his forehead. This tuft was tied erect with a buckskin string, so that it might finally assume that position once so fashionable among the warriors of the tribe. Evidently, he was disposed to cling to custom, and yet I noticed he wore suede oxfords over flashy socks and smoked Turkish cigarettes.

## XIII

NEARLY always after telling a story the Chief would spend a little time talking to Coyote-runs and Plain-bull. I had grown to expect it and used these moments to go over my notes. This time his talk was interrupted by the coming of Plain-feather, a friend of mine whom I had not seen for some time. Plain-feather had once told me a story so crammed with horrible detail that I believed I should be obliged to leave it out of a collection I had made among the Crows for publication. However, after much careful work I had included it, and later on was greatly surprised to discover almost the identical tale in a translation from the Sanskrit. Now I wished to tell him, as best I could, of finding his story in the writings of a very ancient people who had inhabited a far-off land across the Big Water. After we had greeted each other, as he could speak no English, I asked the interpreter to relate to him what I wished him to know. He was intensely interested, and, after the interpreter had finished speaking, stood looking for a long time out of the window across the plains. Then he turned to me, his face expressionless. "These things are beyond us," he said simply. When he was gone the Chief began again.

"One winter," he said, "when I was quite young, not over twenty, Pretty-eagle carried the pipe for a war-party against the Pecunies [a tribe of the Blackfeet, called Piegans by white men]. He was a brave warrior and picked his party with care. He has now gone to his Father, but Bell-rock, who is older than I and was older than Pretty-eagle, is still alive and will remember what I am going to tell you.

"The weather was cold, but in those days in all kinds of weather men had good times. Cold days were the same to us as warm ones, and we were nearly always happy. We headed for the Beartooth Mountains, with only one horse in the party. He carried our extra moccasins, a few robes, and some pemmican, enough for twenty men. Three times we camped in the mountains, and then turned away for the Judith Basin where we stopped for one night in sight of the Two Buttes. Next morning before the party moved, seven Wolves were sent out to travel ahead, and I was one of the seven. Bear-from-the-waist-down carried the pipe for the Wolf party, who were Fleshings, Bird-on-the-ground, Medicine-rock-goes-out, Little-gun, Gros Ventres-horse, and myself. Besides these warriors there was a pup with us Wolves, a young man on his first war-party. His name was Pounded-meat, a brave man of eighteen years.

"We Wolves were on a high hill looking toward Plum Creek, and saw just below us on the plains a band of buffalo cows. Before we had looked over the country carefully, as we ought to have done to see what besides buffalo was there, somebody—I have forgotten who—said, 'We have been eating bull meat long enough. Let us go down there and kill a fat cow, and fill up.'

"Nobody objected, and all except Gros Ventres-horse and me went down the hill to get some fat meat. I suppose I might have gone too, if I had not been the owner of the only telescope in the party, but I stayed to use my glass and very soon was glad I had not left the hill. I saw a queer thing, a thing I had never seen before. A

Pecunie war-party with only one Wolf ahead of it was traveling toward us afoot, through the snow on the plains. And the queer thing, or I mean the thing that made what I saw look queer, was far behind—so far off that without a telescope I might not have seen it at all. It was a Flathead war-party on the trail of the Pecunies! The Flatheads had horses, but were themselves walking in the snow on the Pecunies' trail.

"I was most interested in the Pecunies, of course. They were nearest, and the people we were looking for. Besides, they were heading for the Crow country, but I thought we should soon be able to show them Crows enough, without their having to travel so far. Their Wolf, who was now on a knoll top, stopped, turning back toward his party. This was enough for me, and I howled like a wolf to tell my companions I had seen the enemy.

"I felt certain the Pecunie Wolf had seen only me and not the buffalo hunters down below, who were five against the Pecunie party of exactly that number, but I was mistaken. Before I could reach the trail my companions had made in the deep snow on the hillside when they went down to get a buffalo cow, I saw the Pecunies coming straight for them, and howled again, turning to see how far off our main party was. Seeing our men coming as fast as they could lead the horse along, some of them running ahead, I knew we now had the best of it, and waited for the whole party to come up.

"But the Pecunies, when they discovered us on the hill, turned to run, with the five already down on the plains after them. Most of us dashed down through the snow to join in the chase, but the horse could not walk on that side of the hill, the snow being deeper; so they had to blindfold him and push him over. He slid to the bottom without hurting himself, making a fine trail for those who waited to follow.

"Nobody besides myself knew about the party of Flatheads who were yet far away, but I realized we should have trouble with them after we finished with the Pecunies. We were scattered all the way from the horse to the leaders. The latter were not very far behind the Pecunies, who finally made a stand in a deep wash-out, where they began shooting at the leading Crows.

"We did not have a gun in our party, only bows and arrows. I remember I had twenty good arrows that day, and a bow that would send them where I wished them to go. I had been hoping for an opportunity to count coup, and when I reached the wash-out I found what I wanted. Our party, all that had reached the wash-out, had surrounded the Pecunies, but as yet had done them no harm. There were four of the enemy in a bend of the wash-out not far from me, and one, who had both a gun and a pistol, about two hundred yards further up. This fellow appeared to be the pipe-carrier for the Pecunie party, and I wanted his scalp.

"I tied my medicine beneath the left braid of my hair and sang my war-song. When I had finished, the lone Pecunie in the wash-out stood up. He knew my song! 'Let us not fight,' he called out. 'Let us make peace.'

"Ho! I knew him! His name was The-bull. He had once left his own people, the Pecunies, to live with us. He had taken a Crow woman and then, after a while, left her with children to support. These children yet live on this reservation. I see them quite often. Ho! I knew The-bull. My heart was bad toward him. He had betrayed us and, knowing our country, was even now leading a war-party against us.

" 'I know you well,' I called to him. 'You are The-bull, and this day you shall die!'

"His point of the wash-out bent out toward us, and I saw several large bunches of rye-grass, tall as a man, standing between it and me. Thinking I could use them, I ran zigzag, as the snipe-bird flies, for the nearest.

"The-bull fired, but missed me, and I slid into the first bunch of rye-grass to get my breath. But I was not alone. Somebody's feet touched my shoulders when I landed. Looking back, I saw the Wolf pup, Pounded-meat. He was breathing hard, and his eyes were burning like coals in a lodge fire. I felt proud of him. 'Be careful,' I told him when I stood up to run for another bunch of the rye-grass.

"I slid into it, unhit by The-bull's shot, which spattered snow and little stones around me and Pounded-meat, who was sticking to me like mud. I had again felt the pup's toes against my back when I landed, and now I felt his breath on my neck when I got up on my knees. I was not twenty feet from my enemy, and, if only I could manage to see him, I could finish things quickly from where I was.

" 'Get up and fight me! I am here before you!' The-bull's voice surprised me.

"Though I did not believe him, I raised myself up to look over the top of the rye-grass. And there he was! His gun flashed almost in my face. He missed! And my arrow passed through his nose just above his mouth. Its blow whirled him half round, and he staggered backward, falling into the wash-out and looking as though he held my arrow between his lips.

"I realized his hurt was not fatal and was aware that he had a pistol. He would get up to fight again. Springing to the rim of the wash-out I looked over it, into his pistol's smoke that blinded my eyes. Its bullet brushed my hair, but that was all—all he had time to do before my arrow reached his heart.

"I knew there was now another Pecunie under the bank near me and thought I had him located exactly. But he fooled me a little by moving. If his gun had not hung fire he might have finished me, but he had bad luck and missed. I heard my arrow strike bone in his body before I jumped down into the wash-out with the Wolf pup by my side.

"The-bull and the other Pecunie were finished. I realized there might be others under the banks, which were not so high as I had thought; but as I could see none, I raised my bow to tell any Crow who might see it that the fight was over.

" 'Look out! Here they come!' cried Pounded-meat.

"I turned, an arrow on my bowstring, and saw a gun flash from the wash-out below me. The-wolf, one of our best men, pitched head-first into the snow, and was still. I jumped upon a rock to climb out and go to him. But Pounded-meat held my arm.

"A lone Pecunie was running toward us down the wash-out with Pretty-eagle and another Crow behind him. We pressed our bodies against the bank until the Pecunie had come abreast of us; then Pounded-meat sprang from my side and slapped his face—counted coup—before Pretty-eagle could get hold of him.

"They fell in the snow and rolled over. Somehow the Pecunie escaped Pretty-eagle, and if Little-gun's arrow had not caught him he might have given us a lot of trouble. He was the last. The fighting was finished, but The-wolf, a good man, was lying on the snow in a circle of blood, and our hearts were beside him.

"We raised him up and got the blood out of his mouth. 'Try to save him,' said Gros Ventres-horse to my uncle, Takes-plenty, one of our Wise Ones, as he untied a fine necklace from his own neck and put it around mine." [It was not customary to offer reward directly to a medicine-man for his services. To show earnestness the necklace was given to Plenty-coups, who was related to the medicine-man.]

" 'I will try. We must not leave his body in the Pecunie country,' said Takes-plenty, removing a little buckskin pouch from his shirt.

"The-wolf's mind was yet sound, but he was nearly gone. The bullet hole was in his breast, and blood was coming from his mouth and nose, when Takes-plenty opened his pouch and took out a pinch of The-flower-the-buffalo-will-not-eat [?] and a little of another kind of flower I did not know. He chewed them in his mouth, and, stepping to windward, blew them upon The-wolf's breast. He then walked one-quarter round him and did the same thing, then half round, then three quarters, each time chewing a portion of the two flowers and blowing them upon The-wolf, who lay upon his back with his eyes open. I knew he understood what was going on, and hoped with all my heart he would get well.

"Takes-plenty snorted like a buffalo-bull and jumped over The-wolf's body, and I saw the wounded man turn his eyes and try to move his body a little, as though he wished to sit up. But Takes-plenty did not even look at him. He jumped again and again over his body and legs, each time snorting like a buffalo-bull. 'Bring me a robe with a tail on it,' he said to us, who were watching.

"He shook the buffalo's tail before the seeing eyes of The-wolf, snorting and jumping over his body till The-wolf reached out his hand in a weak effort to take hold of the tail. But Takes-plenty did not even look, or did not seem to. I felt like calling out, 'Wait! wait!' because he did not see and was now even backing away from The-wolf, who reached farther and farther, at last sitting up.

"I stepped out to help him, but Takes-plenty waved me away and kept backing, backing up, his eyes now looking into the dim ones of the wounded man that were growing brighter as he reached out again and again to take hold of the buffalo's tail that fluttered about before them, until he staggered to his feet without help.

"They were walking slowly in a circle, when Takes-plenty, without looking our way or stopping the buffalo's tail that kept fluttering before the eyes of The-wolf, said 'Open his shirt.'

"As I did so, I heard his breath whistling through the bullet hole in his breast. I stepped back, and Takes-plenty, standing a little way from him, told The-wolf to stretch himself. When he did, black blood dropped out of the hole to the snow. When red blood came my uncle stopped it with the flowers from his pouch.

"The-wolf walked alone among us. 'I am all right,' he said, and our hearts began to sing. It was then I thought of The-bull's scalp. My people seldom take an enemy's scalp if a Crow has been killed in the fight. But now that The-wolf was all right I went back and took the scalp of The-bull, the only one I wanted."

Here I interrupted Plenty-coups, to ask about Takes-plenty, the medicine-man who had healed The-wolf. I have heard many such tales, and always from old men. Their replies to my question, "Why are such cures not practiced today?" are the same. Plenty-coups said, "Such things were done long ago by good men who were wise. Nobody now understands what our Wise Ones knew before the white man came to change this world. Our children learn nothing from us, and, watching the young whites, have no religion. I hope, if they cannot find and hold firmly to our old beliefs, that they will learn the religion the white man teaches and cling fast to it, because all men must have a religion, if they would live."

"You said you took the scalp of The-bull," I reminded him, to get him back to his story.

"Yes," he answered. "I was proud to take it to my people. We got three guns and five pistols, besides. But no horses, because like ourselves, the Pecunies were afoot.

"I told Pretty-eagle about the Flathead war-party now, and we got out of there, putting The-wolf on the horse. Snow began falling thickly, and the wind blew a gale out of the north, whirling the dry snow about us, but we finally reached the hills. By midnight we were among the pine trees, and putting out some Wolves, rested ourselves till a Wolf named Little-old-one wakened us near daybreak.

"The Flatheads were coming on our trail, as I had expected, and we lost no time getting along; that is, the main party, with The-wolf on the horse, left at once. Two of us remained behind with two guns to surprise the Flatheads, but we soon learned that the enemy had left our trail and gone around the hills to catch us on the other side. We hurried to tell this to Pretty-eagle, who at once got ready to give them a fight, setting the party in position where it could look downhill every way.

"No snow was falling now. The moon was out again, and very bright, even though the day was not far off. Countless tree shadows, looking blue-black beneath the moon, pitched up the steep hill-side like mighty arrows; and little winds were blowing fine snow out of the treetops. Suddenly I heard a horse snuffle.

"Our three Pecunie guns surprised the Flat-heads so badly that they ran down the hill, the dry snow scattered by their horses' feet sparkling in the moonlight as though the sun shone upon it. We did not wait and pushed on, all except Bear-from-the-waist-down, The-people, and I, who took the enemy's trail to see if they left any blood on the snow. But we found none. We had done them no harm.

"Pretty-eagle now kept to the high hills in spite of the deeper snow there, and we were obliged to break a trail all along for the horse that packed The-wolf, who had several accidents on the way. Once a low-hanging limb brushed him from the saddle so that he rolled down a hill in the snow. But he got up by himself and was laughing when we helped him back on his horse. I was glad to see our own country again. As soon as we were decently in it we killed some fresh meat, kindled a good fire, and got nice and warm. Nobody was missing, and I had the scalp of The-bull.

"When we saw the Crow village on Two Creeks not far from Sweetgrass, we knew that the clans had gathered, by the large number of lodges. Our hearts sang with the thought of visiting friends we had not seen in a long time. We did not wish to enter without making a show; so I went in myself to the village and got some horses to ride, and we had a big time riding about, telling of our fight with the Pecunies and firing the guns we had taken. There was a big time that night. So many women asked me for the scalp of The-bull that I had to cut it into many pieces to make it go as far as I could among them. All night they danced with it. Their hearts were very bad for The-bull, who had left a Crow woman, and now they felt they were even with him. But while the women danced to the war-drums I went to sleep, my heart singing with them. I had again counted coup, and my name was on the lips of everybody at the scalp-dance."

The Chief said he wanted his pipe, and while Plain-bull filled it for him, Coyote-runs said to me: "That woman, the one The-bull ran away from, is living here yet. Her name is Many-lodge-doors. I often see her, and she sometimes speaks to me of the night when she danced with the scalp of her runaway man."

"I have not finished with the Pecunies," said Plenty-coups, taking the pipe. "The next morning, when the village moved, snow was falling and the air was sharp as a knife. We who had been on the raid against the Pecunies rode together beside the line of moving travois, singing our war-songs, while young women smiled at us and called our names. It was good to live in those days.

"Suddenly we saw the horses far ahead stop, and men ride out from the head end of the line. One came dashing back along it, calling out some message, but we did not stop to hear it. We lashed our horses into a run to see what was going on, hope for a fight in our hearts. We got our wish. Men were already fighting on the Sweetgrass [creek], and we saw a dead Pecunie, without his scalp, lying on the snow ahead of us.

"Big-nose, who was on a fast horse, and ahead, leaned over as he went by and struck coup on the scalpless one, he being first to fall in the fight. Nobody halted, and just as Big-nose struck his coup I saw a Pecunie sitting on the ground ahead. I think Big-nose discovered him at the same time. Anyway, after striking the dead Pecunie he raced away for the man on the ground, who, although armed, could not stand because of a broken thigh.

"Things told as I am telling them now do not seem to be fast, but they were very fast while they were happening. Big-nose intended to count a double coup and jumped from his running horse beside the Pecunie to take his gun. As he sprang toward him the fellow fired, and Big-nose fell with his own thigh broken.

"They faced each other, each with a broken thigh, neither able to stand, Big-nose wholly unarmed because he had thrown away his gun when he jumped from his horse so that he might count a fair coup. I saw the Pecunie raise his knife and saw Big-nose back away, pushing his body along with his hands.

"I lashed my horse! The Pecunie was edging himself toward Big-nose, who was backing off, each pushing himself along with his hands, the Pecunie's knife always ready. Big-nose was working toward his gun, but it was far away, and he dared not turn his head to keep from circling [going in wrong direction]. And the Pecunie was gaining. I expected to see him throw his knife into the body of the Crow.

"How slow this sounds in spoken words! There were several men behind me, but I did not know it then. I saw only Big-nose, backing in a circle that would never bring him to his gun.

He must have heard our horses coming because he gave the Crow war-cry without taking his eyes off his enemy, who was edging along after him with his knife.

"We circled around them, not daring to shoot for fear of hitting Big-nose. The Pecunie knew he was gone now, and gave the Pecunie yell. Several bullets cut it short. I never knew just whose bullets struck him, of course, but that Pecunie was a good man, and brave.

"We did not stop there long. A band of Pecunies had crossed Sweetgrass and had thrown up a breast-work of willows in the brush. Our warriors had twice charged and had been beaten back, losing several men. When we arrived we all charged again and were driven back, with Bobtail-raven shot through the breast, rather low down, and Shot-in-the-hand wounded in the shoulder.

"The best shooting had come from a point in the breast-works where I had seen a Pecunie wearing a white man's hat. I made up my mind to try to get him. Dismounting, I stripped and tied my medicine beneath my braided hair. I knew mine was a desperate game, but I played it, sliding safely to the foot of the breast-works, where I waited to get my breath. To shoot me now the fellow with the hat would have to stand up and lean over the breast-works, and I did not believe he would risk it. I knew he was right behind the breast-work from me because I saw his coup-stick leaning against it. Its feathers waved in the wind over my head, and when I had rested a little I took hold of it and pulled. He hung on, but I got it away from him, and when I saw his face over the brush I struck it with his own coup-stick.

"This started things in our favor, and the Crows charged, only to find nobody behind the breast-works. Burnt-eye shot my man with the hat, as he was following his friends into the willows. However, I had already counted a beautiful coup on him, and with his own coup-stick. The Pecunies had killed three Crows and wounded several. We had four scalps, and of course did not know how many we hurt. We Crows had counted three coups: one by Big-nose, which I have told you about; one by White-bull, who struck the Pecunie breast-works while under fire; and mine. I have finished for today."

## XIV

THUS abruptly the Chief terminated his story and turned to talk to an old man who had entered a little before. Sage thrashers whistled and called among the bushes and box-elders along Arrow Creek, and because the hour was early and dinner a long way off, I sat down to watch these attractive birds which do not come so far west as the Rockies. The Crows call them The-bird-that-makes-many-sounds, and old Cold-wind once told me that a white man had offered him one hundred dollars to find a nest of the sage thrasher. He said he had often looked but had never found one. This seems strange to me, since the bird must nest in the Crow country where in summer time he is plentiful. Even if Cold-wind spent but little time searching for nests, it proves the sage thrasher a wary bird, because an Indian generally knows all birds and animals that inhabit his country; and if the sage thrasher were not uncommonly cunning Cold-wind would have had no trouble in winning the hundred dollars.

On my way to my quarters I flushed a covey of pin-tail grouse. Cold-wind had told me, I recalled, that when Old-man-coyote made the bird he used the muscles of a buffalo-bull for its body and a wolf's claw for its beak. Tough material for the making of a toothsome bird, I think.

Across from my quarters I heard a little child crying on the road, and beheld a spring wagon drawn by a span of pinto horses. A Crow woman was driving, her head so wrapped with bright-colored silk handkerchiefs that, above the rattling of the wheels on the stony way, she could not hear the screams of the little girl running behind. I called loudly and pointed to the child, whose wails ceased as soon as the team stopped. The woman looked back and began to remonstrate rather violently, but in the end the child won her way and climbed into the seat beside the woman. The latter whipped up at once, in time to make way for a Crow warrior who was going in the same direction in a Ford car without fenders.

Plenty-coups began his story next morning by pointing out a few of the white man's frailties. "By the time I was forty," he said, "I could see that our country was changing fast, and that these changes were causing us to live very differently. Anybody could now see that soon there would be no buffalo on the plains, and everybody was wondering how we could live after they were gone. There were few war-parties, and almost no raids against our enemies, so that we were beginning to grow careless of our minds and bodies. White men with their spotted-buffalo [cattle] were on the plains about us. Their houses were near the water-holes, and their villages on the rivers. We made up our minds to be friendly with them, in spite of all the changes they were bringing. But we found this difficult, because the white men too often promised to do one thing and then, when they acted at all, did another.

"They spoke very loudly when they said their laws were made for everybody; but we soon learned that although they expected us to keep them, they thought nothing of breaking them themselves. They told us not to drink whisky, yet they made it themselves and traded it to us for furs and robes until both were nearly gone. Their Wise Ones said we might have their religion, but when we tried to understand it we found that there were too many kinds of religion among white men for us to understand, and that scarcely any two white men agreed which was the right one to learn. This bothered us a good deal until we saw that the white man did not take his religion any more seriously than he did his laws, and that he kept both of them just behind him, like Helpers, to use when they might do him good in his dealings with strangers. These were not our ways. We kept the laws we made and lived our religion. We have never been able to understand the white man, who fools nobody but himself. However, even with all our differences, we kept our friendship for him, as I shall show you.

"One winter day when the snow was deep, our Wolves came in and told us the Pecunies had stolen many of our horses. I was camped with about forty lodges on Rock Creek, and our horses were running in the hills where they could paw away the snow and get grass. Because of the slow days that had come to us with the white man, and the lack of long grass to cut with our knives, we had no good horses tied near our lodges ready for trouble, as we always had had when the buffalo were plentiful. We had to go out in the hills and catch horses to ride. That is the way we lived now, like a lot of sleepy people whom anybody might whip.

"Eight of us went out and caught up our best

horses, the fastest and strongest. We expected the trail to be a long one, and kept wondering if white men would stop us from getting back our property. Anyway we started, and picked up the Pecunie trail on Elk River. The water was frozen, so we crossed on the ice in the face of a cold wind that kept it wiped clean of snow, which had drifted into piles out on the plains and along the river banks.

"Where Park City now stands we came to a few houses, and the white men who lived in them told us the Pecunies, or somebody, had taken most of their horses too. We talked to them as best we could with signs and a little English (when we knew it was nearly right), and at last four white men who had lost good horses wanted to go along with us to get their stolen property. I believed them able to take care of themselves and agreed, which was one of the most foolish things I ever did.

"They began to show me this soon after we started. Their horses had been eating hay and oats in a house, while ours had been pawing snow for grass in the windy hills. Naturally their horses could travel faster than ours, but because the trail was likely to be a long one I tried to hold the white men back, telling them to save their animals for the trouble ahead. They would not listen but rode on, while we walked, until their animals grew tired. Then the white men camped. When I passed them by their fire they wished me to stay with them, but I told them the Pecunies would not camp and that if we expected to catch them we must keep going. I explained to them, as best I could, that the thieves were driving nearly one hundred horses and would be unable to go so far in a day as we could, if we kept at it. This did no good. They said their horses were tired out, and of course they were, having been ridden all day in the deep snow. So I left them, wishing with all my heart that I had not sent four of my men back to the Crow village when these white men joined me to go after the Pecunies.

"They caught up with us late the next afternoon, and at once began to talk about camping and eating, but this time I pretended not to hear them at all. I kept pushing on with my three men—Plain-bull, who is with us here, Strikes-on-the-head, and Big-sky—thanking luck that no more than four white men were in our party. I saw they were a hindrance instead of a help, and that, if left to themselves, they would never in this life catch a Pecunie horse thief.

"In the middle of the night we came to the headwaters of the Musselshell, and when the Seven-stars [Big Dipper] had turned clear around Ek-kha-ceh-say [North Star] I saw that two of my men were far behind because of the condition of their horses. I knew I should have to give them rest, and stopped to look for a good place. The wind had blown the ground bare of snow where I was standing. I signed all to stop while I looked a little farther, before camping.

"It was well I did so. I had gone but a little way when I became suspicious of a place in the rim-rock where the snow was piled about some boulders, and, stooping low to get the sky between me and the rim-rock, discovered some horses above it. Besides, I smelled a little smoke that was from a fire nearly dead. The Pecunies were near it, I knew.

"Not daring to trust the white men to do the right thing, I hurried back to where they were waiting with Plain-bull. 'Stay here,' I signed to them. 'I will go ahead now and steal their guns before we attack them, if I can.' But I could not hold my white friends. They were unmanageable, and got on their horses to charge the camp in that dim light.

"I ran ahead, waving them back, but they followed on horseback and began to yell. Yes, I am telling you the truth; they began to yell, and I dodged behind a boulder, leaving them out there sitting on their horses and yelping like coyotes.

"They did not shout long. The Pecunies were not fools. I soon saw rifles poking over the rim-rock, one of which spurted fire. Down went a white man with a bullet over his eye.

" 'Go back!' I called, making the sign. But my words did no good. There they sat on their horses, wearing too many clothes and looking foolish, until another tumbled off his horse with a ball in his forehead. This time the two others moved a little. One jumped from his horse and hid behind a boulder to fight. He was smarter than the others, but just as he poked his rifle over the boulder a bullet struck the rock and glanced into his face. Ho! The lead bullet split and spattered, making a terrible wound that knocked him down in the snow as though finished.

"I looked to see what the other was going to do with himself and saw him running away afoot, as fast as he could go. Next I saw him stagger and fall, get up again and run, and then tumble. I thought he stayed there.

"I would have helped him if I could, even though I thought him worth very little. My two men were coming up now and getting themselves into position to hold the Pecunies from getting away. I had not yet got a shot. Bullets chipped pieces from my boulder every time I stuck my head above it, and I had to be careful. Those Pecunies did good shooting that morning. I kept them wasting their ammunition by making them think my robe was my head, while I watched for a shot at a tall Pecunie who, I knew, had done most damage to the white men. He had seen the two Crows join us among the boulders, and probably thought more were coming and that it was time to move from where he was. I was expecting him to make a run for different cover, but when he did I missed him clean, shooting too low. My bullet made him duck behind another rock that was not so good as the one he had left, and I made ready for him to come out again. When he did, I doubled him up.

"The others saw him fall, which made them wish to move to the rocks higher up on the hill. When they started I made one of the best shots I ever fired, killing one of them halfway up that hill, as easily as though he had been just against my gun barrel. One of the others, who had a Winchester, began a lively spurt of shooting now, but they were in a tight place, and knew it. Their guns were faster than ours, but ours carried bullets farther and could reach their position, even in the higher rocks. However, our own were accomplishing no more than theirs; so, after stationing two of my men to hold the Pecunies where they were, I crept back with Plain-bull to see what we could do for the white man whose face had been smashed.

"We found him breathing like a snorting horse and bleeding badly. We carried him to a safer place, dragged the two dead men together, and then went to look at the trail left in the snow by the white man who ran away and fell down. We followed his tracks only a little way, looking carefully for blood, saw where he had fallen and got up, found where he had tumbled again and then floundered to his feet to run on. He had not been wounded, only scared; so we came back to the job of trying to get the other Pecunies among the rocks.

"On our return we stopped again by the side of the wounded man, and while we were kneeling down to see if there was anything we could do for him, we heard horses coming—a dozen or more of them. We stood up, but not for long. White men began to shoot at us.

"I waved my hand—made the sign for 'friend' —but they did not understand and kept shooting. Their bullets were kicking up the stones around us and we feared they might kill the wounded white man. We dragged him behind a boulder to save him from being finished by his own people, and hid ourselves to think. We were in a bad situation, with white men shooting in front and Pecunies shooting behind us. We thought if we shot up the hill at the Pecunies the white men would understand that we were friends. But when we tried this it did no good. The white men's bullets kept clipping against our boulders. Some other thing had to be done quickly.

"I tied a white piece of buckskin on my wiping-stick and stood up unarmed. Holding my stick high with my right hand, I stretched my left above my head, so that anybody might see that I carried no weapon. In this manner, expecting to be shot down, I began walking toward those men, and more than one bullet *was* fired at me before they stopped shooting. They at last realized that I was only one man, and unarmed, and that I could not possibly kill them all. When I got near enough to speak my name in English, fortunately one of them knew it. This ended the trouble and we shook hands.

"I led them to the spot where their friends were and, as best I could with signs and a very few English words, explained what had happened. While some of them were examining the wounded man and the dead ones whose bodies were now frozen very hard, two white men went out to find the man who had run away. So Plain-bull and I started again to see what we could do toward killing the other Pecunies. [Pecunies—often spelled Pikunis—means "painted-face," though their enemies declare the word to mean "*scabby*-face."]

"We crept up the hill from rock to rock, while Big-sky and Strikes-on-the-head kept up their fire, until we came to the tall one's body. Here

Plain-bull stood up and, walking to the tall one, counted coup on him in the face of the firing up the hill. I took the fellow's scalp, and together we set out once more to get the other whose body was still farther up the hill. But the white men now began calling and beckoning us. They had promised to keep up a fire while we did this, but now when they began calling and beckoning they quit shooting. We turned back, leaving that Pecunie unscalped. I have felt sorry ever since.

"The white men had built a large fire, and also they had gone out and killed a white man's cow, so that they might have meat to eat. All those white men seemed to think about was eating and camping. But we Crows were hungry too, so we ate meat with them, while the Pecunies made good their escape. I wished I had a few more Crows with me instead of those white men.

"While we were eating, the whites who had gone to follow the one that ran away came back with the coward. He was unhit. Two bullets had struck his fur overcoat, and one had knocked him down on the snow. He had got up running and hadn't stopped for a long time.

"I myself had three holes in my capote and one in my shirt, but my skin was not even scratched. We rounded up all the horses and helped the white men pack their dead on gentle animals. Their bodies were so frozen that they broke them across the backs of the horses so that they could carry them away from there. I led the party back to Park City.

"The weather was so cold that the trees popped and snapped, and more than once we were obliged to stop and build fires to warm the white men, who wore too many clothes. The snow in places was drifted very deep, but never did we unload the horses that carried the dead. Many times since then I have remembered how strange the stiff arms and legs looked in the clear moonlight, especially when we were among scattering trees. They did not please me, I remember.

"It was a hard journey for those white men. Two whole days and nights, with little rest, took us to Park City, the white men's village, and it was there I learned that white women mourn as ours do. My heart fell to the ground when I heard them crying and wailing for their men, who need not have died if only they had used their heads a little. I do not like to fight with white men.

"We left their horses at Park City, coming on back to our village, which of course had moved while we were gone. Only one lodge was standing where we had left it, and that belonged to the father of Plain-bull, who waited there for his son's return. I shall never forget how the old man got up and danced around his lodge when

I told him that his son had counted coup."

I asked for the names of the white men who had accompanied him against the Pecunies, but he could not give them. He said, however, that the white man who had been so badly wounded in the face lived long afterward in Park City. "He was young then," he told me, "and had more sense than his friends. I do not believe he is much over sixty years old, if he still lives."

He smoked awhile, and I asked him if he had ever made fire by friction with sticks. He said he had, but that it required strong hands, and time. "Two men are better than one when fire is made by rubbing sticks," he smiled. "The match is a wonderful thing. I never light my pipe or a fire with a match, but that I remember when flint and steel was the only way we knew; and even that came to us from the white man. Before that we made fire by hard work."

Mr. Asbury, the superintendent of the Crow reservation, came just now to draw up some papers with the Chief, who wished to leave forty acres, including his house, to the tribe as a park. He had driven a long way, and I prepared to forego work for a day and leave the old man to arrange his affairs with the superintendent. But that gentleman very graciously told us that he would come another time, and left us to go on with our story-telling.

# XV

HAVING wondered where Plenty-coups got the idea of leaving his house and adjoining lands to his tribe for a park, I asked him. It was borrowed from Mount Vernon.

"Many years ago," he told me, "I stood beside the tomb of the first white Chief, George Washington, and felt glad to be there. I had heard much about this Chief, and had noticed that no man spoke harshly of his life or deeds, and that all held his name in reverence. I was one among many visitors at Mount Vernon that day, and yet there was no talking, no noise, because people were thinking of the great past and the unknown future. When people think deeply they are helped, and in the silence there I sent my thoughts to the Great White Chief in that other life. I spoke to him, and I believe he heard me.

I said: 'Great Chief, when you came into power the streams of your country's affairs were muddy. Your heart was strong, and your tongue spoke straight. Your people listened, and you led them through war to the peace you loved. They remember your words even to this day, are helped and made strong by them. As you helped your people, help me now, an Absarokee chief, to lead my people to peace. I, too, have a little country to save for my children.'

"I felt then that he heard me, and I have not changed my mind. Mount Vernon is very beautiful. People travel far to see it. I planned then to leave my house and some land around it, as a park for my people. I wish the title to rest with the tribe itself, and not with any clan or society. I have spent my life here. This spot was shown me in my great medicine-dream, and I want my people to possess it forever, just as white men own and keep the home of their great Chief, George Washington."

His speaking of Washington, and perhaps the use of the match to light his pipe, seemed to turn him to speak of prophecies made by his tribesmen, and thereafter he spent the afternoon recounting these, often telling at length the dreams of men who had lived long before him. Some of them are remarkable and leave one wondering if their visions came wholly to the Crow prophets in dreams, or were inspired, in some measure, by chance meetings with white men or Indians who had seen or heard of the latest attainments of white civilization. The Crows saw steamboats on the Missouri River very early, but this could not have led them so far as to foretell railroads, flying machines, and many-storied buildings where white men "lived one above another."

Medicine-raven, a close friend of Plenty-coups, had such a dream in the Crazy Mountains, and it was so baffling in its mistiness that even the Wise Ones could not interpret its meaning. Many years passed before the Crows understood the great dream of Medicine-raven, who lived to see some of his dream's prophecies come true, but died before "wagons traveled in the air," as they did when he dreamed in the Crazy Mountains, at the age of nineteen.

Old Indians have told me that dreams foretold the coming of white men years before they appeared on this continent, and that even the clothes and weapons of the strangers had been minutely described by men who saw them in their dreams.

I was unable to turn the Chief back to talk of himself. Prophetic dreams occupied his mind, and at last I gave up for the day, going back to my quarters on Arrow Creek. Near Pryor I met Chief Bell-rock, who is eighty-five, and alert in both mind and body. He leaned far from his pony to shake my hand and tell me that his heart sang because of our meeting. "I shall not see many more snows," he said, his kindly face almost happy. I experienced the feeling, which always comes to me when an old warrior speaks of leaving this life, that Bell-rock believed he had lived here wisely and well, and that plentiful reward awaited him beyond. There is never any shadow of doubt in these expressions by old Indians concerning death and a future life. They do not merely imply belief, but carry the positive declaration, "I know!"

Next morning, going to the house of Plenty-coups, I cut across Arrow Creek, and, skirting a half-mowed meadow, came upon a dozen Indian boys swimming in a deep hole gouged into the grassy flat by the late high water. They had not seen me and were lively as frogs, their lithe bodies glistening in the sun as they raced around the edge of the pool. I might have watched them longer, or I might have slipped away without disturbing the party; but, instead, I coughed loudly and stepped out beside the pool. What a stampede! I caught flashing glimpses of lean, naked bodies disappearing into the bushes where nettles grew plentifully, and stood for a moment gazing down upon scattered raiment, meager enough, and ranging from leggings to store trousers and shirts. The pool, so suddenly relieved of its visitors, was roiled somewhat, and its surface disturbed. It reflected my shadow protestingly. I heard gleeful giggling in the bushes beside the creek as I turned away.

When near the Chief's house I saw a horseman turn in at the gate. At first I thought him a white man, reflecting that white men always disturbed us. But when the rider dismounted I knew he was an Indian, Coyote-runs.

"I feared you were a white man," I told him, after greeting Plenty-coups, who sat with Braided-scalp-lock under the trees. "But when I saw you get off your horse, I knew you were a Crow." [Indians dismount from their horses on the right or off side.]

The Chief laughed at this, and I saw that I had, by good fortune, touched a responsive chord in his memory. "We have learned many things from the white man," he said. "Some of them are good, but the off side of a horse is the natural one for us, and we have not changed our way of mounting or dismounting. Habit is strong with all men, and even when they borrow customs to fool others they become careless, so that natural habits give them away."

He turned to Coyote-runs, spoke rapidly and

with glee, reminding him of some incident; then he said to me: "The white man, even with all his smartness, cannot long make his trail look like an Indian's, any more than an Indian can fool his own people by pretending to be white. Both will at last forget the game they are playing and do some natural thing. Then they get caught.

"Once upon a time in winter I went to the mountains with Sharp-head and Big-sky to kill mountain sheep. They were plentiful then, and we stayed but two nights on the hunting grounds. The second night I had a bad dream. I knew something was wrong in our village on Rock Creek, and by daybreak we were packed up and traveling toward it.

"Somebody had stolen about a hundred head of our horses the night before, and the thieves were believed to be white men. As they had left one boot-track in a patch of snow, I went out to look at it. It had been made by a white man's boot, right enough, and there was only one imprint to judge by. No Indian wore boots, but the track seemed to me to turn in a little at the toe. The man had mounted a horse just there, on the near side as a white man does, and yet the boot-track did not turn out enough at the toe to make me certain the horse thieves had been white men. I searched for another track but there was none, so at last I gave up, calling a council to talk things over. The country now had many white men in it, and we feared they might object to our chasing horse thieves wherever their trail led.

"All except myself believed the horses had been taken by white men and that our property was gone forever. 'I will dream,' I told them. 'Go back to your lodges. Stay there till morning, unless I call you in the night.'

"After a sweat-bath I plunged into the icy river and then slept. Near midnight one of the Little-people came to me in a dream. He stood at my feet and said: 'My son, you were in the mountains and have come back to gain a good bay horse and a pinto. They shall be yours if you follow the trail of the Sioux who have robbed you.'

"I knew then that the boot-track had been made by an Indian's foot, and that we should retake our property. I called out, and men came again to my lodge. 'Get your fastest horses,' I told them. 'We shall look for the thieves' trail at once.' "

The old Chief's story of the chase was minute in every detail. Finding where the stolen horses had been driven across the ice on the Yellowstone on dirt scattered so that the animals might walk more easily, the Crows followed northward until they reached a few log houses built on the present site of Billings. Here they learned that a gray horse and saddle had been stolen. This made their cause common with the whites of the little village, and a letter addressed "to all white men," vouching for his character and the worthiness of his mission, was written and given Plenty-coups, who now believed he had a warrant to follow the thieves wherever they went. Such letters were often written years ago when the country was changing from wilderness to settled communities. I have more than once written them for Indians myself.

"I do not believe those white men would have given me that letter if they had not hoped I would bring back their gray horse," smiled the Chief. "You see the ground was frozen so that any trail was difficult to follow," he went on, "and white men are not used to such work. However, a hundred horses make a sign that is easily followed over any ground, and we found where the thieves had camped on the present site of Huntley. They were two whole days ahead of us. So we hurried on until, in the afternoon, we came upon a place where they had stopped to let the horses eat grass a while, near the mouth of a little box-canyon [steep sided, like the sides of a box]. Not once did I see a boot-track all this while, although I searched wherever such a sign might show itself. Late that evening we came to a bunch of culls [inferior horses] the thieves had cut out of the stolen band and left in a little canyon between the Elk River and the Musselshell. Forty head of these were strong enough to travel, and I sent all but Bell-rock back to our village with them.

"In another day's ride Bell-rock and I found a few more culls at the mouth of a box-canyon that had been barricaded against pursuers, but we left them to pick up coming back. I discovered another boot-track at the barricaded canyon, but still thought it turned in too much at the toe to belong to a white foot. Bell-rock, however, yet felt uncertain what manner of men we were following, red, or white. My dream had told me the thieves were Indians—Sioux—and that we should overtake them. They were traveling more slowly now, while we were gaining on them all the time. Still, nothing had shown us positively by sign whether they were white men or Indians.

"Finally, when the sun was nearly out of sight, we saw smoke. It came from their old campfire, but they were gone. A half-burned log told us we were still half a day behind them. At this place too, while looking for more sign, we picked up a white man's coat, a hat, and a pair of trousers. They did not fool us much. White men wear too many clothes and never leave any off their bodies in cold weather. The clothes settled the question for me, but Bell-rock still believed the thieves might be white men; and we both disliked the thought of trailing white men in a country where they were so plentiful. I got off my horse to feel in the trousers pockets, knowing nothing would be in them, and as I did so, beheld an offering to the thieves' medicine hanging on the limb of a tree. It was a small bundle of red cloth, and some tobacco.

"Now we laughed! Now we danced! Here was proof that the men we were following were red like ourselves, and Sioux at that. My heart began to sing. Two of them would be riding the good bay horse and the pinto, which the Little-person had spoken of in my dream. They would be mine, and I should be paid for this trouble by getting back my property. The foolish Sioux had given themselves away. They could not wait to reach their own country to offer cloth and tobacco to their medicine, but, even when wearing a white man's boot to fool us, had offered it while we were on their trail. You see? They forgot and did the natural thing, just as all men do after a while. But I had felt certain after seeing the first boot-track, anyway, and my dream had assured me they were Indians. Whenever a man pretends to be somebody else than himself he does not last long.

"We passed another camp where they had

killed a white man's cow, and had even stopped to dry some of the meat a little over their fire. By this we knew they believed themselves safe and would grow more careless. Not far from the mouth of the Musselshell we came to a house. A white man and a Crow woman lived there. The man's name was Long-hair [Carpenter?], and he gave us food. The woman said she had heard many horses pass the house the night before. I told her that when we returned we should be very hungry. 'I will fire two shots if it is night, and by them you will know who has come,' I told her. Then we rode on.

"We knew long before this that there were four men with the stolen horses, and their trail told us we ought to catch up by dark. When the first star came into the sky, Bell-rock pulled up his horse and turned to the wind. 'I smell smoke,' he said.

"We got down to walk, following the smell till we saw a little fire blazing in some willows. When we drew close we could see a Sioux putting dry wood on the fire that sent up sparks as though telling us it was glad we had come. I might easily have killed that Sioux, and I wished to, but Bell-rock objected. 'They are four to two,' he whispered, 'and besides I would rather have our horses than a Sioux scalp.'

"I knew he was right, even while I was thinking what a fine mark for my rifle the man by the fire made. He had long, nicely braided hair and wore better clothes than we did. I have never forgotten how much I wished to send him to his Father. White men ruled the country now, however, and might not think I had done right in killing the Sioux—and besides there were our horses. We might lose them if I fired a shot.

" 'Good!' I told Bell-rock. And in almost no time, without disturbing their guards, we had rounded up not only our own horses but the Sioux's. After we had driven them a little way, and while Bell-rock kept them going, I went back to the Sioux camp. I did not wish them to have to guess who had beaten them at their own game, so I split a willow stick, thrust into it the letter the white men in Billings had given me, tied some red cloth to the stick, and stuck it in the ground where the Sioux must see it when they looked for the horses. Of course they would not be able to read the letter, any more than I could, but they would carry it to some white man who would tell them what it said, and then they would know who set them afoot in the Big Dry.

"The stars were sparkling in the sky, and the wind was on my back, when I caught up to Bell-rock and the horses. The way was far, even to the house of Long-hair. Almost the first thing I did when it was light enough to see, was to look for the two horses the Little-person had described; and there they were, just as he had said, a bay and a fine pinto. Of course I had known they would be there, without looking.

"It was past the middle of the night when we saw the black-looking house of Long-hair, like a great rock on the plains. The running horses clattering over the frozen ground set a dog to barking near the corral, and a horse whinnied as though greeting friends. I fired two shots, and a candle-light flickered through the glass window in the house. We were safe. A rest would give us strength, besides helping the horses. I shall never forget how good that woman's Crow words sounded at the door of that white man's house, nor how kind she and her man were to us. They helped us corral the band, fed the horses great piles of clean hay, and gave us food and a bed where we slept like dead men until long after the sun came.

"When we were ready to go on, Long-hair and his woman went out to the corral with us, where we gave them two good horses. To play even they sent one of their cowboys with us to help drive the band. This man was very kind, cooking for us when we camped and making coffee that had plenty of sugar in it. But when we arrived at the Elk River we let him go back, ourselves pushing on to Billings, where we gave the white men the gray horse. They never recovered their saddle, because we had not been able to get it from the Sioux without a fight—and perhaps we should not have got it even then. Not once did we permit ourselves to become careless, though so near our own country. We had done well and did not propose to lose what we had gained. The bay horse, I now saw, had once belonged to the Crows. His old owner often tried to trade with me for him, but because of my dream I kept him until he died of old age."

As he always did after telling a story of adventure, Plenty-coups here expatiated on the days of his youth, laughing jovially with Coyote-runs and Plain-bull over some incident; and then, as though remembering the present, he sobered.

"Those were happy days," he said softly. "Our bodies were strong and our minds healthy because there was always something for both to do. When the buffalo went away we became a changed people. Meat-eaters need meat. Other food is strange to them. Idleness that was never with us in buffalo days has stolen much from both our minds and bodies. When I think of buffalo meat I am hungry, and I think of it often. The buffalo was not only our food but our clothing and shelter. The other animals furnished only a change of meat and summer clothes. The buffalo was everything to us."

He could not be turned from this vein of thought, but dwelt on feasts of buffalo meat as a child speaks of a picnic. "My mouth waters when I remember the meat-holes," he said. "We used to dig a hole in the ground about as deep as my waist. You have seen many of them along the creeks and rivers. We would heat little boulders until they were nearly white and cover the bottom of the hole with these stones. Then we would cut many green boughs of the chokecherry trees and cover the hot stones a foot deep with them. Upon these we would place thick chunks of buffalo meat, fat and fresh from the plains, sprinkling them with water. On top of the meat went another layer of boughs, then more meat, more water, and so on, until the hole was full. Finally we spread the animal's paunch over the hole, covered it all with its hide, put gravel on this, and kindled a log fire. Men kept the fire going all day and all night yet never burned the robe. The next morning when we opened the hole to feast, even the birds of the plains were made hungry by the smell of the cooked meat. Every bit of good in the buffalo was in the pit. Little was wasted except the horns. I have made myself very hungry telling you this. I will talk of something else to forget meat-holes."

His description had been so detailed that it had made me hungry too. The smell of meat cooking in the house had never before seemed to me so inviting, and I looked at my watch,—only eleven o'clock and the Chief, anxious, as he had said, to forget meat-holes, was telling another story.

## XVI

"ONE day when the summer was growing old, Big-shoulder and I were east of the Little Bighorn, scouting for Sioux. They had been trying to steal Crow horses, and we had not located their camp. Late in the afternoon, however, we saw their lodges and crept close enough for me to kill a Sioux warrior before riding back to our people with the news that not only were the Sioux in our country, but also Cheyenne and Arapahoe.

"As our people did not wish to fight them, we moved our village over here on Arrow Creek. But the enemy followed, and early one morning our Wolves brought in word that we should soon be attacked by more than twice our number. We could not run, even had we wished to go farther, burdened as we were with our women, children, and horses. There was nothing to do but stand and fight.

"How the voice of a brave man can strengthen the hearts of others! Iron-bull and Sits-in-the-middle-of-the-land were our head chiefs. They rode through the village, each on his war-horse, each speaking to our warriors and even to the women whose hearts were on the ground. 'This is the day to go fighting to your Father,' they told us. Those words sent my blood racing through my body. There was no rushing about, no loud talking. Even the women's faces told us that they would do their part. Men did not hurry; and, because there was now no chance for surprise, caught their best horses and stripped their own bodies to die fighting. While we painted ourselves the drums kept beating, and our women sang war-songs. No man can feel himself a coward at such a time. Every man that lives will welcome battle while brave men and women sing war-songs. I would have willingly gone alone against our enemies that day. But almost before we were ready to meet them they were coming—they were in sight.

"We swung our lines around our village, riding out from it so that bullets would not reach our lodges. I have never seen a more beautiful sight than our enemy presented. Racing in a wide circle, Sioux, Cheyenne, and Arapahoe gave their war-cries and fired at us from their running horses. But they were not near enough. Their bullets fell short. Iron-bull had ordered us not to fire a shot until the enemy was very close, and then to aim at the middle of the mark, just where a man's body sits on his horse, so that our bullets would kill or cripple either horse or rider. At the shooting by the enemy our line halted. Our village and we ourselves were inside the line of the enemy, who did not come any nearer, but kept circling and wasting bullets. But he made a fine show with his beautiful bonnets and fast horses, some of them our own.

"Inaction was beginning to fret me, when a young Sioux dashed from their line. He rode straight at us until he was within easy rifle range; then he turned his horse and rode him along our line, his feathered war-bonnet blowing open and shut, open and shut in the wind, as he swung his body from one side to the other on his horse. He was riding a beautiful bay, with a black mane and tail, and fast.

"Two shots spurted from our line, and down went the bay horse and the handsome Sioux. Both shots were as one; there was but one report, and Little-fire [who has just died] lifted his gun high. 'I killed him!' he cried. But Gun-chief, far along the line, said, 'No, no! It was my bullet that doubled that fellow up!'

"All this time the man was not killed at all. He was running by now, and Swan's-head was after him to count coup. The race was short. I saw a feather fly out of the Sioux's bonnet when Swan's-head struck with his quirt, saw the Sioux stagger under the blow, turn about and fire, with his gun's muzzle almost against Swan's-head's breast. The Crow reeled on his horse but did not fall, sticking to his horse to reach our line, with a big bullet through his breast. I saw a piece of his lung sticking out of the hole in his back, and he was bleeding so badly that his horse was red. His eyes were dead.

"With a yell that was good, He-is-brave-without-being-married darted after the running Sioux, who was now close to his friends. I saw the Crow strike him and count his coup fairly; but even as he struck him, the Sioux shot He-is-brave-without-being-married in the breast, just as he had shot Swan's-head. He was a brave man, that Sioux, and a good fighter.

"It was now that Iron-bull, our chief, ordered me to charge with forty men. I headed straight for the running Sioux who had shot two of our men. He reached his friends before we caught up, but we broke through their line and turned its ends, losing only one man in the charge. My own line was scattered. Seeing the handsome Sioux running to catch up and mount behind a man riding a white horse, I gave chase, hoping to catch him and count coup on him, but before I could come near him he had climbed up with his friend, who lashed the white horse to get away.

"I struck them both with my rifle barrel, and both fell, the one behind backward to the ground. He was the one I wanted. I whirled my horse to ride him down, but he got up and fired. He missed me but he killed my horse, which fell on us both.

"Dodging his struggling hoofs, I reached out to catch the Sioux, but failed. When I got up he was running again, and his friend who had fallen with him was a long way ahead.

"He would have escaped without a scratch if my uncle, Long-horse, had not come up just then. He let me take his horse, and I raced after the man who had done so much damage.

As we ran the Sioux shot Crazy-wolf, who was giving chase with me. Crazy-wolf went down between the Sioux and his friends, who were being driven back by the Crows; and, fearing the Sioux would try to take his scalp, I rode hard to prevent this. The Sioux stopped only long enough to take the Crow's gun and then ran on; but not for long. He heard my horse behind him, and when he turned to look I shot him dead. He was very tall, and one of the best fighters I ever saw.

"The fight had now left me behind. Our warriors were driving the enemy away, and on both sides of Arrow Creek the Sioux, Cheyenne, and Arapahoe were being whipped. I forgot to tell you we had help that day. There were forty lodges of Nez Perce visiting us when the enemy attacked, and their warriors helped us, as they should have done under the circumstances. The Nez Perce were not always friendly to us. There was sometimes war between us. But this time they were our friends, and always their warriors are brave men. If it had not been for them we might have been badly whipped ourselves.

"As it was we lost a good many men, and so did the enemy. However, we took over two hundred head of their horses and, as soon as we were able moved our village to a better position, expecting another attack. Swan's-head, who was still living, I helped to hold on a horse as we moved. When he breathed I could hear his breath gurgling in the bullet holes, but he knew what was going on around him and spoke to me in his right mind.

"After we had set up our lodges on the south bank of Elk River, and before many had been pitched, I saw Hunts-to-die, Medicine-wolf, and Bird-shirt, our Wisest Ones, talking together about Swan's-head. By and by I was told that Bird-shirt had said he would try to cure his wounds, and my heart sang.

"The three Wise Ones who had been talking together stripped as though to go into battle, and by speaking to Swan's-head, revived him while a large brush lodge was built near the river. They carried him into this lodge and laid him down, though I was sure his eyes could now see nothing and that he was nearly gone.

"A crier now rode through the village, whose lodges were not yet half up. He told the people they must form a way from the brush lodge to the water in the river, that this way must be kept open, that nobody must cross it and no dog come near it, and that perfect silence must be kept by everybody. But he said that anybody might stand beside the lines that formed the way to the water and look on, if he wished to.

"Quickly our people formed the open way.

No dog was permitted to come near it, and there was silence—not even a whispered word was heard. We could hear the wind in the leaves that covered the brush lodge and the sound of the water running in the river, but nothing else until the medicine-drums began to beat. I could feel them. They made me think deeply. When Bird-shirt began to sing, I wished to sing with him. But I dared not, and stood silent beside the line that made the way to the water, while the wind brought me the odor of burning sweetgrass in the lodge where my friend was lying on the ground. The voice of Bird-shirt rose and fell with the drums, keeping with it, as though each was the other's friend. I could look into the lodge, and even see Swan's-head and Bird-shirt. I saw the Wise One take his medicine from its bundle. It was a whole wolf's skin with the head stuffed. The legs of the skin were painted red to their first joints, and the nostrils and a strip below the eyes were also red. I watched Bird-shirt paint himself to look like his medicine-wolf skin. His legs to the knees, his arms to their elbows, his nostrils, and strips below his eyes were made red, while he sang steadily with the beating drums. He painted his head with clay until it looked like that of a buffalo-wolf, and he made ears with the clay that I could not tell from a real wolf's ears, from where I stood. All the time he kept singing his Medicine Song with the drums, while the people scarcely breathed.

"Suddenly the drums changed their beating. They were softer and much faster. I heard Bird-shirt whine like a wolf-mother that has young pups, and saw him trot, as a wolf trots, around the body of Swan's-head four times. Each time he shook his rattle in his right hand, and each time dipped the nose of the wolf skin in water and sprinkled it upon Swan's-head, whining continually, as a wolf-mother whines to make her young pups do as she wishes.

"I was watching—everybody near enough was watching—when Swan's-head sat up. We then saw Bird-shirt sit down like a wolf, with his back to Swan's-head, and howl four times, just as a wolf howls four times when he is in trouble and needs help. I could see that Swan's-head's eyes were open now, so that he could see Bird-shirt stand and lift the medicine-wolf skin, head first, above his own head four times, whining like a wolf-mother. I seemed myself to be lifted with the skin, and each time there was, I saw, a change in Swan's-head. The fourth time Bird-shirt lifted the wolf's skin, Swan's-head stood up. He was bent, his body twisted, but his eyes were clear while Bird-shirt trotted around him like a wolf, whining still, like a wolf-mother coaxing her pup to follow her.

"Bird-shirt walked out of the lodge, and when Swan's-head followed him I could scarcely hear the drums or the men's voices singing his Medicine Song. I felt that I was with Swan's-head when he stepped once, twice, three times, and then into the open way to the water behind Bird-shirt, who kept making the coaxing whine of a mother wolf, until both had stepped into the water.

"Not once all this while had the drums stopped, or the singers, whose voices rose and fell with the drums. Everybody was watching the two men in the river.

"Bird-shirt led Swan's-head out into the stream until the water covered his wounds. Then he pawed the water as a wolf does, splashing it over the wounded man's head. Whining like a wolf, he nosed the water with the wolf skin, and made the nose of the skin move up and down over the bullet holes, like a wolf licking a wound.

" 'Stretch yourself,' he told Swan's-head; and when Swan's-head did as he was bidden, stretching himself like a man who has been asleep, black blood dropped from the holes in his chest and back. This was quickly followed by red blood that colored the water around them, until Bird-shirt stopped it. 'Bathe yourself now,' said Bird-shirt, and obediently Swan's-head washed his face and hands in the running water. Then he followed Bird-shirt to the brush lodge, where they smoked together. I saw them.

"Our Wise Ones learned much from the animals and birds who heal themselves from wounds. But our faith in them perished soon after the white man came, and now, too late, we know that with all his wonderful powers, the white man is not wise. He is smart, but not wise, and fools only himself."

Swan's-head died three or four days after Bird-shirt had treated him, his death being attributed by the Chief to a violation of one of the orders first given to the people. Plenty-coups made it quite plain, however, that while the violation of this order was not wanton, the Wise One had detected it before entering the brush lodge to smoke with his patient, and that he rebuked the people for their carelessness, telling them there was then little hope for the complete recovery of Swan's-head.

## XVII

TWO old men having come now to arrange for the burial of the aged warrior who had died that day, I left them with the Chief and went out to the spring to eat my lunch. The little boy with one good arm and the tiny girl who lived with Plenty-coups had built a small lodge near the water and were playing at being their natural selves, their horses meanwhile cropping the grass as though they, too, enjoyed the game. I did not disturb them but went farther down the meadow to a grove of box-elders, where a pair of robins scolded me while I ate. I could hear the drum of Bear-below, and wondered again if the old man had given his life to the instrument. It was beating almost continually night and day while I was there, and long since it had aroused my curiosity. But asking the reason would have availed me nothing. Perhaps none but Bear-below himself could have answered, and I did not know him well enough to ask. He was, no doubt, making medicine, though for what specific purpose I did not learn.

Back at Plenty-coups' house I found the company waiting, but without impatience. Coyote-runs was telling a story. When he had quite finished the Chief said to me: "Now I will tell you a story that will show you how powerful my medicine was in war.

"I have explained that to keep other tribes out of our territory we sent clans to its four points to tell encroaching men they might hunt on our lands if afterward they would go away to their own parts again. One of these clans sent us word that the River Crows had been attacked by Crees and Yanktonese Sioux, who together had killed several men, besides taking a band of horses from our brethren. We did not wait, but started out to find and fight the enemy.

"The berries were red and weather was very hot. We swam the Big River, running right into a large camp of Red River half-bloods, who were killing buffalo. They were badly frightened, but after we had assured them we were not at war with them, they gave us some meat and tobacco, besides telling us where we might find a large Sioux village east of them.

"Of course our Wolves had seen the half-blood camp with its high-wheeled carts and countless dogs that were half wolf, but our main party had not, so that when we came out of the river right into it we frightened them enough to make us laugh; and the meeting even startled us a little. They had every kind of woman, from every tribe. We soon found one who could speak Crow as well as talk signs. We were glad of the news they gave us, but did not trust them very much, telling them plainly that if they sent any messenger to the Sioux village warning them of our coming, we would hold them responsible and punish them. This made them careful not to ride too far from their camp for a while.

"These mixed-bloods of the Red River were a tribe of people to themselves. Neither red nor white, they traveled and camped together, wearing bright-colored white men's clothes mixed, like their blood, with the regular apparel of our own people. Their habits were more nearly like ours than like those of white men, except that they used Red River carts drawn by horses, carts that squeaked and screamed across the plains like a herd of crying things looking for rest. And they packed dogs often, just as our fathers did before they got horses to carry their things. Their women were either full-bloods from the different tribes they visited or half-bloods like themselves; and no tribe made war against them, though none trusted them as friends or allies in times of bad trouble.

"The next day we located the Sioux village,—three large circles of lodges, one inside another, set on a flat near the Big River. We were a large party and there were many good men among us, so that now when we saw the enemy's village we stopped to smoke and talk things over. It was decided to send our Wolves at daybreak to try to stir up the Sioux and get them to follow the tormenting Wolves into a trap [an ambuscade]. The trap was quite a way from the village, and our Wolves were told to approach the enemy closely, kill one or two if possible, and then fall back fighting as though they depended only upon themselves, until they finally reached the thick bushes where our main party was hidden.

"I was one of these Wolves chosen to stir up the Sioux and lead them into our trap. I had the privilege of calling my men, because I carried the pipe for the first party, and I chose Bull-that-does-not-fall-down and Covers-his-face to go with me. I remember that Goes-against-the-enemy and Scalp-necklace also led parties of Wolves that morning. Scalp-necklace always wished to be called for such service. He had a grudge against all our enemies and was always trying to get even with them. His face had been so badly broken in battle that he wore a strip of buckskin over his chin to hide it from sight, and every scalp he took he hung on that piece of buckskin until it was all scalps. Still he was constantly looking for another. He was a man who did not care when he went to his Father.

"These little Wolf-parties left our camp one after another, so that when the Sioux attacked the first they would meet another, and another, thinking these scattered Wolves were a war-party by themselves. I do not remember how many there were, but I guess twenty went out that morning to stir up the Sioux, while three hundred Crow warriors waited in the bushes to finish them.

"But our trap was too far from the village. I knew we should have a hard time to get the Sioux to follow us that far without getting caught. A man never knows that his horse is faster than his enemy's until he tries, and when we stirred up the Sioux we should have to ride for our lives. But we were out to get them started.

"A creek running into the Big River was between us and the village, and looking through the willows that were thick on its banks I could see in the upper end of the lodges a party of young warriors smoking in the shade of a shelter set up against the sun. I was near enough to hear them laughing. Farther up I could hear people in the river taking a swim. By leaving my horse with my two companions and crossing the little creek, I thought I might creep near enough to shoot one of the young warriors and still get away by running.

"I decided to try this and crept to the edge of the brush. One foot was in the water and I was standing up, when two shots rang out on the hill we had just descended. I drew back into those willows more quickly than I can tell you, and stared up on the hill. A Crow was riding up there, making the sign "retreat" [riding his horse back and forth].

"Plainly something had gone wrong, and I must get out of those willows with my two men. There was no time to fool away, if our party had changed its plans, and I started at once. But at the edge of the willows on the side next the hill, and off the hill itself, I discovered a Sioux coming straight for us. 'Back,' I whispered to my companions, who knelt among the willows. The heated air was so still that sage-hens coming down to the water held their wings away from their sides. I could see the heat dancing on the grass tops ahead of the oncoming Sioux, who was bare-legged, on a fine roan horse. He must have thought the two shots had been fired by a Sioux hunter, because he kept right on coming toward us.

"When he was almost in range I raised myself up and aimed my gun, holding it there ready while I waited for him to come a little closer. While I waited, a horse whinnied in the village across the creek, and a man spoke to another over there. Then I fired. The Sioux fell with my bullet through the calf of his leg; and his horse was crippled too. My bullet had broken its front leg near its body. Both began to hobble toward the village, with Bull-that-does-not-fall-down after them to count coup. But the man got away, and of course the horse was no good any more.

"I rode up the hill and fired two shots at the swimmers in the river. I saw my bullets splash water among them, but as my horse was afraid of my gun, I did miserable shooting all that day. Still my shots at the swimmers were like sticks poked into a hornet's nest. Sioux began to come out, plenty of them too, and I rode down the hill with Covers-his-face, stopping at the bottom long enough to kill the crippled horse before we raced off, with Bull-that-does-not-fall-down just behind us.

"Immediately ahead I saw four more Crows and urged my horse to catch up with them. Now we were seven, with bullets kicking up the ground under our horses. I looked for a place to make a stand, but could discover none until we came to a buffalo-wallow where two other Crows had stopped. One of them was named Red-wing; the other's name has slipped from me. We rode into that wallow with them as if it were the best spot on the world.

"While we were making ourselves as safe as possible in the wallow, I caught a flashed signal [mirror signal] on a butte a long way ahead, which said, 'Come in. Enemy too strong.' My people had evidently seen more Sioux than they wanted.

"I was willing enough to do as the signal said, but I could not move now. We in the wallow were surrounded. Each of us held tightly to his horse's rope, knowing that to be set afoot now meant certain death. The Sioux charged, and we drove them back. When their line broke, I saw a good chance and ordered my men to ride at them, nine against a hundred. And in spite of such odds, we drove them away, coming back to our wallow with two scalps.

"But I thought again of the flashed signal. I was holding my men against orders, and they might be killed. I made up my mind to let six of them go, and sent them to catch up with our main party if they could, leaving me with two others in the wallow. Our position was well known to the enemy and I had no reason to believe they would let us alone, but I felt that if we all left it to go to our friends, the Sioux would have nothing to do but follow us. Now we in the wallow furnished them a job that might take their minds from the ones who had left us there to try to reach our main party, which I was sure had stopped on Wolf Mountain.

"We watched several parties of Sioux pass, just out of our range, and were beginning to wonder that they did not attack us, weakened as we were. Midday came, and we heard heavy firing far ahead where we knew our friends must have been forced to make a stand. The sun was so hot that even while standing still in the wallow our horses dripped sweat, and lying flat on the ground we three panted like running wolves. Why did not the Sioux attack us and give us something to do! Waiting there in the hot sun was wearing us down. I made up my mind that if the Sioux would not attack us, we would attack them.

"When the next party came along, out of range like the others, we fell in behind them and gave them something to think about besides our friends ahead. But suddenly we saw them turn and ride toward us until they were nearly in range. Then they split into two parties, riding past us out of range, with many more coming—

all doing as they had done, avoiding us altogether. They might easily have ridden us down, but they feared my medicine! It was very strong that day, and if my horse had not been so gun-shy, I might have taken more scalps than the one I got.

"We at last caught up to our main party, which we found had suffered little. They had taken some horses from the Sioux, who had killed and scalped old Scalp-necklace after he had scalped two of them. There was another loss too. One of our men in the main party had accidentally shot his own horse in drawing his rifle from its scabbard when the Sioux attacked on Wolf Mountain."

There is nothing improbable in this story to one who is acquainted with the Indian. The respect for big medicine by all the plains tribes is well known, and yet to the uninformed their superstitious belief in its power to render its possessor invulnerable must be beyond understanding. The early white trappers not only fell into the red man's custom of carrying medicine-bundles themselves, but in battles with Indians used every possible ruse to establish in the minds of their foemen the belief that the white men's medicine was the stronger. Success in this has often been wholly responsible for victory over great odds. But let an Indian see a Sign, feel in the presence of danger that his own medicine is adequate, and he will stop at nothing.

Probably because of his bold attack from the buffalo-wallow, which broke their charging line —nine against many—the Sioux in this instance believed that Plenty-coups was invulnerable. His medicine was powerful, they were sure, and therefore they avoided further conflict with him. The old warriors of all the tribes I know tell such stories of days when their medicine gave them victory over odds, and these men always attribute their successes to their medicine far more than to their own prowess.

## XVIII

THE story-telling was nearly over now. The Chief's wife, who had been lying in the shade where she might hear it, was called away by a visitor. A Crow woman wearing bright-colored clothes drove up to the gate in a spring wagon, and stopped. After helping her bright-eyed little girl to the ground, she climbed down herself and tied the team, pausing leisurely to watch two Indian boys racing on ponies along the road she had left. The Chief's wife got up to welcome her, and with her and the little girl went into the house.

"When I was twenty-seven," said Plenty-coups, "we had another fight with the Sioux, and this time we fought to help the white man. There were soldiers at Fort Maginniss over in the Judith country, and one day we went there to trade some buffalo robes for tobacco and cartridges. We pitched our lodges on the Judith River, and had been there three days when one of our warriors, who had just returned from the white man's fort, told us that the soldiers had been attacked by our old enemies.

"The sun was past the middle of the sky when we started for the Fort, but long before we reached it the fight was over, and the Sioux had gone away with nearly all the soldiers' horses. Besides this the Sioux had killed and wounded several white men.

"We looked around the Fort to learn what the country could tell us, and found a stand of coup-sticks stacked with the feathered ends up. This told us that the Sioux felt themselves to have been victorious and were only through for the day. Whoever carried the pipe for them expected to return and fight again; so our Chief, Long-horse, called for men to go out and meet them. 'All who will follow me against the Sioux stand to one side,' he said, 'and those who are not going had better give their moccasins and leggings and ammunition to those who are.'

"More than a hundred men stepped away from the crowd around the Sioux coup-sticks, while others began to take off their moccasins and pick their cartridges out of their belts. My uncle, White-horse, gave me everything he had, even his shirt; and Plain-bull's brother gave me his belt half full of ammunition, so that I had all I needed for a long fight.

"We did not go back to the village, but took the Sioux's trail from where we were, following Medicine-raven, Mountain-wind, Red-wing, and Long-horse all night. As we lost the trail in the darkness, at daybreak I climbed a high hill with my glass. Looking back the way we had come, I saw the Sioux between us and our village. It was plain that when we had turned southeast in the night we had passed them—gone around them—so that now we were between them and their own country. They were already moving when I saw them, not toward the Fort, as we had expected, but toward us, as though they intended going back to their own lands.

"To tell my friends I had seen the enemy, and that he was coming, I howled like a wolf three times. Then I ran down the hill to our camp, where I found our men already on their horses, stripped, and painted for a fight. I had counted the Sioux, and while I was getting myself ready told Long-horse there were about one hundred and fifty of them, and that they were driving their horses in seven bands, five herders with each.

"I was on my war-horse and moving out with most of the party when Mountain-wind called, 'Wait!'

"Stopping with the others, I saw Mountain-wind take his buffalo-neck shield from its buckskin cover and hold it above his head. Mountain-wind was going to talk to his medicine before the fight. The shield had the figure of a man painted in blue on its face, a man with large ears and holding in his left hand a red stone pipe that was straight. [Straight pipes are sometimes used in their ceremonials.] The figure was in the center of the shield, whose rim was bordered round with beautiful eagle feathers that fluttered in the breeze.

"Mountain-wind began to sing words we could not understand. They were his Medicine Song, and strange to us all. But each time he finished it we gave the Crow yell, until he had repeated his song four times; then we gave the Crow war-whoop, so that the enemy might hear. We believed he was through now, and would have dashed away, but his queer actions held us.

"He was staggering like a man who is dizzy, and singing softly to his medicine, his face not toward the enemy, but toward the rising sun, like the raven in the mountains. And his shield was moving, waving, just as a man's hand moves when, in signs, he is asking 'What?' of somebody.

'What is going to happen?' he was asking the sun, while he still staggered toward the east, like a man blind in a strange country.

"My eyes would not leave him, even when I thought of the Sioux. Suddenly I saw him drop his shield! It fell to the ground face downward, and when he lifted it he did not turn it, but raised it to the level of his breast, with its face downward, as it had fallen. And he kept it level, held it still, while every eye in our whole party watched it, watched him, scarcely hearing his softly sung Medicine Song, till an eagle's feather from the shield's rim fell fluttering to the ground.

"Then Mountain-wind turned the shield to see its other side. I did not breathe while he looked at the face of the blue man painted on it. 'I see many Sioux scalps,' he said, his voice sounding like one who has just awakened from sleep. 'And many horses, more than a hundred,' the far-off voice of Mountain-wind went on, 'but one great warrior is not going back with us,' it was saying.

"Then Long-horse began to sing: 'Today one of us is not returning home. You are all guessing who this man may be. I can see a great darkness coming from the east. It will be slow in reaching our country, but some day it will darken it for our people. I do not wish to live to see this change that is coming. Have no fears for yourselves. It is I who will not return home with you today.

Feel no sadness. Remember that nothing is everlasting except the Above and the Below.'

"We would rather have heard any other man sing that song, and our hearts fell down when its words ended. But Long-horse seemed happy enough, and sent four Wolves toward the enemy to tell us when to charge.

"But these four Wolves were so anxious to count coup they forgot all about us. We were watching them, however, and when we saw them mount and ride forward we followed. This was signal enough for us; and we surprised the Sioux, who broke quickly. The fight became scattered, each man for himself.

"I chased three Sioux on better horses than mine, before I saw another dodge behind a tree, afoot. He had a bow, and I got off my horse to fight him. When he showed himself a little I fired but missed him, and he sent me an arrow that barely let me live. Every time I poked my head from behind my tree that Sioux was ready and sent an arrow that made me dodge before I could shoot. Not until the Sioux discovered another Crow coming at him did he give me a chance to kill him. When he stepped out a little to shoot an arrow at the other man, my bullet sent him to his Father.

"He was a good man, that Sioux. There were five arrows sticking in my tree just level with my head when I got him. But he was not the coup, not the first Sioux killed. It was another Sioux, who had sent Long-horse to his Father, that was the coup. I did not see who killed him, but I remember it was Back-of-the-neck who struck him and counted coup. I remember, too, that this other Sioux was very brave and handsome. But he made our hearts fall to the ground when he sent Long-horse, our great Chief, to his Father.

"The fighting was fierce. The sun was in the middle of the sky before it was finished. We had nine scalps and all the horses. But nothing could pay us for Long-horse, who was gone. He had well known he was the feather that fell from the shield of Mountain-wind. Never shall I forget how his song saddened me, nor how we felt while we carried his body home.

"Our village had moved up to the Fort of the white soldiers, and when we rode into it there were many white men among the lodges. But we did no singing, did not show off. There was no dancing that night, I can tell you. Our hearts were heavy and our faces painted black for Long-horse, who was worth all the Sioux that ever lived.

"His son, who had been with us and had seen his father fall, came now to plead. 'Dance,' he said. 'Be merry. My father would have it so. Be glad of our victory. Lift your hearts. My father would not have you mourn for him.' But though we tried to please him because of his father, our hearts refused to sing for us, and the women wailed all night.

"The next morning the white soldiers picked out their horses and each gave us a blanket or some cartridges, whatever he wished to part with. We did not care what horses they took, or what they gave us for bringing them back. Long-horse, our great war-chief, was no longer with us, and we could think of nothing else."

Plenty-coups dwelt at length on the loss to the Crows of Long-horse, recounting stories of his wonderful leadership in war. Two other old men had joined us under the trees, one very much wrinkled and blind in one eye. I watched their saddened faces while the Chief told me that, after delivering the stolen horses to the soldiers, his people had wandered to the Sun River, where for a time they mourned, killing only enough elk to eat. "It was not until we heard that Elk River was freezing that we cut a supply of lodge poles and came back here to Arrow Creek to kill buffalo for the winter's meat," he said, as though finally dismissing thoughts of mourning.

## XIX

"EVERY man among us was burning to get even with the Sioux," Plenty-coups went on, "and as soon as our meat and robes were gathered against the cold weather, one hundred of us set out to avenge Long-horse. The weather was bitter when we crossed the Elk River below the mouth of Bighorn and went into camp on The-place-where-the-colts-died (Tulloch Creek). Our chiefs were Medicine-raven, Bear-wolf, and White-strip-across-the-face.

"Carrying the pipe for the Wolves, I came across an empty camp of the enemy on the Rosebud. He had built brush lodges there, and by these I saw he outnumbered us. But to learn how many warriors were in the Sioux party we Wolves waited until our own men came up, and then had them go into the brush lodges. When they were all inside there were still nearly as many lodges unoccupied, so that we judged the Sioux outnumbered us nearly two to one. Their trail pointed into our own country; so there was no good in turning back. The Sioux were out to make war on us, and now were between us and our friends. It was our duty to follow them and attack them in the rear, if we could.

"In one of the brush lodges our chiefs held council. The pipe was finally handed to Bird-shirt, who accepted it without hesitation. I thought he felt glad of the opportunity, and watched him as I had that day when he led Swan's-head into the river.

"The night was already dark, but I knew it would soon be even darker. By the light of the little fire in the brush lodge where he sat with the chiefs, I saw Bird-shirt strip and paint his body as he had that day when Swan's-head was shot,—his arms to the elbows, his legs to the knees; and there was red under his eyes. He covered his head with his wolf's skin, so that its ears stuck up like those of a wolf, and went alone out of the lodge into the darkness. I saw his gun and knife lying on the spot where he had sat [like the wolf he went unarmed]. Following a little way, I saw him sit down on the trail of the Sioux, just as a wolf sits. There was nothing on his body except moccasins and the wolf skin which was only on his back and head. He howled like a wolf, and then came back and spoke to all of us. 'I will come to you four times tonight,' he said. 'When you hear a wolf howl four times in front of you, listen well, and you will hear other wolves around you.'

"Then a Wolf [Bird-shirt] trotted away on the trail of the Sioux, and the order came for all to follow. We led our horses. It was now so dark that I often put out my hand to feel for the man ahead of me. There were not even stars in the sky, and the cold made our horses shiver. I could not tell how old the night was, but it must have been past the middle when I heard a wolf howl. I stopped, wondering if the howl was really a wolf's. The man behind me bumped into my horse, who snorted in my ear. I could hear wolves howling on all sides of us, and, reaching out to feel the horse ahead, I touched nothing at all. There was nobody there. Though I had stopped the leaders had not; and now I walked fast to catch up, saying nothing about this to those behind me. Three times this thing happened, and I found myself waiting for the fourth time as a man waits to drink water when he is very thirsty.

"At last it came, and the leaders stopped so suddenly that nearly everybody bumped against the horse ahead of him. Wolves were howling everywhere, and one walked past me so closely

I might have touched him with my gun. I saw him quite plainly and heard him whine around our leaders, but whether the thing that passed me was Bird-shirt or a wolf I could not tell—and I was twenty-eight years old, and a chief.

" 'Give me my horse.' I knew that voice. It was Bird-shirt's. One of our men who was back of me brought up the horse. 'We are on a hot trail,' said Bird-shirt. 'The Sioux have divided their party. One division has gone toward the mouth of the Bighorn, the other toward the mouth of the Little Bighorn. This is the largest. Let us travel fast.'

"I felt a bit chagrined when, instead of choosing me, the chiefs called Bell-rock and Fighting-bear to act as Wolves and sent them ahead, but I did not complain. We traveled as fast as we could until we came, near day, to the point where the Sioux had divided into two parties, and then took the trail of the smaller bunch toward the mouth of the Bighorn. Bird-shirt's medicine had told him the truth. On the east fork of The-place-where-the-colts-died our Wolves came in and told us that some Sioux were sleeping in a brush lodge ahead, and that the lodge was guarded by two Wolves who were watching the country, nine in all.

"This brush lodge was near the edge of a deep wash-out. We were close to it when the Sioux were wakened by their Wolves. I saw them running toward the wash-out from the lodge, as we charged it. Hoping to strike coup on the lodge, I pressed my horse; but Fighting-bear had a faster horse, and it was he who struck it. By this time four of the Sioux who had been in the lodge had joined the Wolves in the wash-out, and three more were standing on its edge. I fired at them, and at the report of my gun two of them jumped down into the wash-out, leaving one on the rim, who shot at me; and I killed him. He fell backward into the wash-out where now not a head showed above the rim.

"The Sioux could go up or down the wash-out, and might escape. To head them off and hold them, a party of our warriors rode each way, but only one of the enemy had moved. He was running toward the creek, away from the wash-out. I tried to catch him, but Hillside shot him and took his gun before I got fairly started. There was now no enemy in sight. All the Sioux were in the wash-out, and to drive them out we should have to fight from its edge.

" 'Whoever strikes the edge of the wash-out with his coup-stick shall count coup.' Medicine-raven had scarcely spoken these words when both Goes-against-the-enemy and I raced for the wash-out, afoot. We were side by side when a bullet knocked my companion down. He fell against me, even as I struck over the wash-out's edge with my coup-stick.

"Goes-against-the-enemy had been shot with a pistol. I saw it flash in the Sioux's hand immediately in front of us, and grabbed the man's wrist, falling flat. I held on however, trying desperately to pull the fellow out of the wash-out, but instead he pulled me in. I fell upon him and should have been finished quickly if Strong-heart had not jumped down beside me. His arm was broken just below the shoulder by a bullet, and hung dead by his side, but with his knife in the other hand he flew at two Sioux who were trying to get a shot at me. It was soon finished now. I had plenty of help. Only one Sioux got away. We had eight scalps and several horses, but we did not feel that Long-horse was yet avenged."

He was silent a moment, his eyes looking far off. "I never knew a man who loved to laugh as well as Medicine-raven," he said slowly. "He carried the pipe for us many a time, and he was always successful. White men called him 'Medicine-crow,' just as they call us Crows, who are Absarokees."

My interpreter, Braided-scalp-lock, spoke to Coyote-runs and to Plain-bull, who both laughed. Though I caught the Crow name of the late Hon. Paul McCormack of Billings, I could not understand what they had said about him, and asked.

"We are trying to get Plenty-coups himself to tell you a story about old Medicine-raven," replied my interpreter, "but he says he doesn't want to. He thinks it indecent."

I then asked for the story myself, through Braided-scalp-lock, and reluctantly the Chief told the following:

"You know about Fort Pease? Well, Yellow-eyes [Paul McCormack] used to live there with Major Pease. They built the Fort for a trading post, and they had a hard time keeping the Sioux from killing them and burning the Fort. We all liked Yellow-eyes, especially Medicine-raven, who often paid him a visit.

"Medicine-raven loved a joke, and would work very hard to make a good one because he liked to laugh. I was with him once when he made a joke that nobody laughed at, except himself. He made it for Yellow-eyes, his friend, who told me afterward that he did not sleep for two nights on account of that joke. It was not a good one, and you will not laugh at it, any more than did Yellow-eyes. But I will tell it, because you ask me, and you had better not write it down.

"The Sioux had nearly wiped out Fort Pease [below Billings, on the Yellowstone], and because they were our old enemies and in our country, we took their trail. The weather was bitter cold, so cold that the tails of white men's cattle were frozen off close up to their rumps, and the smoke of our lodges was white in the air. Medicine-raven carried the pipe for us, and we found the Sioux near the Black Hills, and fought them there. We killed six and scalped them without losing a man, so that our hearts were singing when we reached Fort Pease again. We believed we had done the white men a service, and we were cold and hungry.

"But the gate of the Fort did not open, and we saw that the white men were going to fight us, because they believed us Sioux. We fired our guns into the air to let them know we were Crows before they should kill some of us who were their friends. At last, just as we had begun to move away to save trouble, Yellow-eyes recognized our leader, his friend, Medicine-raven.

"This was enough. The gate opened wide, and we rode inside. The white men were very glad to see us, and when we got down from our horses they crowded around us to shake our hands. Yellow-eyes ran straight to Medicine-raven, and, hastily pulling off a mitten, reached out his hand.

"We were all suffering from hunger and cold. Medicine-raven's buffalo robe was wrapped tightly about his body, and he only stuck out a hand which Yellow-eyes grabbed as though he was glad. He shook the hand very hard. When Medicine-raven turned around to shake the hand of Major Pease, I saw Yellow-eyes spring backward and drop something in the thin snow, that sounded like a stone. I looked. It was the frozen hand of a Sioux! Medicine-raven had cut it off a man he had killed in the fight near the Black Hills and had carried it many days to make a joke on his friend Yellow-eyes. But his friend did not laugh."

Not once while telling this incident did Plenty-coups show merriment. His face was stern, and he spoke as if he did not relish what he was saying. However, the story brought him pleasant memories, which seemed in some measure to compensate him.

"I remember that day very well," he said softly. "The white men gave us coffee to drink, and it had plenty of sugar in it."

## XX

"DID the Pecunies ever burn the grass on the Crow buffalo range?" I asked, to start him on something else.

"No," he said emphatically. "The Pecunies are crazy enough, but no red man would do such a thing as that. He would know that he might himself starve if the buffalo did not find grass to eat, and would not burn grass to spite another man, even his enemy."

But I had known of the use of fire in war by Indians, and I asked: "Did your people ever use fire to fight your enemies?"

"Yes. Twice I have known of the use of fire

in war by my people. Once, when I was too young to remember anything well, the Crows surrounded a band of Pecunies near the spot now occupied by the city of Red Lodge. They were in thick willows, and our warriors could not drive them out. There was grass among the willows, and a high wind, so that a fire started in the dry grass soon drove the Pecunies into the open where they were finished by the Crow warriors, who were many times their number.

"The other time our people used fire I was seven years old, and I remember what was said among the men. The Hairy-noses [Prairie Gros Ventres] got into our village to steal horses, and were driven out and surrounded in some willows not far from this place—just over there by the spring where Cuts-the-bear's-ears lives now. When daylight came they killed several Crows who tried to drive them out, and our warriors saw that something different had to be done. Thick grass grew among the willows, and at last the Crows set it afire. But when the flames drew close to the enemy, one of their Wise Ones sang his Medicine Song, putting the fire out with rain. I was too young to know much about it, and what I am telling you now came to me from others who were older. I do know, however, that Bull-lodge, the Wise One who sang and made rain come, was a very powerful man. Our chiefs finally called the

Kicked-in-the-belly clan to drive the Hairy-noses out of the willows, and after a desperate fight the thing was done. But I remember it cost more than it was worth."

"Who was the most powerful Wise One in your own time?" I asked.

"One of the most powerful men I ever knew was The-fringe," he replied. "I have seen him do wonderful things. Though I was very young when he had his great dream, I remember it well enough. Our village was in the Bighorn basin, not very far from Oo-tsche-dea [The-snow-melting-wind-river] where the country is beautiful and the mountains are high. There is a spring in that country which we call Medicine Water because it heals the sick, and it was there The-fringe had his great dream.

"The Medicine Water lies at the foot of a little hill, and in the center of the water, which nearly boils, there is a small island. The-fringe went there to dream, reaching the island by walking a pole which two friends helped him place from the shore. Then, because he requested it, his friends went away and left him on the island, going high up into the mountains to dream, themselves. They could see The-fringe on the island from their beds, but, looking down the third morning, found him gone. A cloud of fog hung over the Medicine Water, hiding all the island; but even when the sun came and drove it away, The-fringe was not there. Something that lived in the Medicine Water had taken him away. But, as they had promised The-fringe before leaving him that they would not do so, they did not go near the spring until the morning of the fourth day. When they at last drew near the Medicine Water, they saw him, not on the island where they had left him, but on the shore itself.

"Nothing could live in the Medicine Water, and there was no way The-fringe could reach the shore and live. Yet there he was, standing alone in the sunshine on the shore, the morning of the fourth day. When they came near enough to speak to him, he held up his hand and they stopped, half afraid.

" 'Go to the village,' he told them, 'and tell the Wise Ones to gather together. Have them build four medicine-sweat-lodges in a row from east to west. They must use one hundred willows in making the first one, and none but the last must be covered until I am there. Tell them also to make plain medicine-trails from the door of each, through the sweat-lodges, to the west, and when they have finished to send for me.'

"His friends did all he asked them. And when The-fringe entered the village he called eleven Wise Ones, and with them smoked in the first sweat-lodge. Then he led them to the fourth, which was covered, and said, 'Roll one hot stone inside, and burn some e-say upon it.' When the Wise Ones had done this, The-fringe told his dream.

"He said that on the first and second nights on the island the hot Medicine Water had washed his body and burned his skin, but that he had not moved or cried out.

" 'On the third night a Person came to me,' said The-fringe. 'He had matted hair and looked strong and not very good-natured. He told me to stand up and follow him, which I did.

" 'He sank beneath the boiling Medicine Water, and I followed, feeling no hurt. We came at last to a great painted lodge that was red and black in stripes up and down it, and I saw many horses near. The lodge was tall, even considering its great size. An Otter was on one side of it and on the other a White Bear. Both were angry because I was there and spoke crossly to me; but the Person said, "Be quiet! This is my son," and neither the Otter nor the White Bear spoke again while I was there.

" 'We entered the striped lodge, the Person and I, and because it was daytime in there, I could see very plainly. "Look about you, my son," said the Person, walking around the fire, where right across from me I saw his woman sitting.

" 'She was strangely handsome, and tall. When she smiled a little at me, I knew she was very kind, that her heart was good. But she did not speak or make a sign to me, and while I stood there looking and wishing she would do one or the other, the Person said, "This is all, my son. You may go now."

" 'I felt sad at the Person's words, but had turned to the door to go outside when the woman asked, "Why do you not give this son of yours something he may use to help his people, some power for good, if used by a good man?"

" 'I thought at first the Person did not hear her. But at last he picked up a strip of Otter skin and a picket pin and gave them into my hand. "Take these, my son," he said in a voice so kindly that I was not certain it was his own.

" ' "And will you give him nothing else?" asked the woman across the fire. "Will you tell him nothing?"

" 'The Person smiled. I saw his face change greatly. "Women are kind," he said, and took me by the hand. "I will tell him that this water will heal the sick among his people, if they will use it," he said, leading me out of the striped lodge that was red and black.

" 'When I wakened I was not on the island where I had made my bed, but on the shore bordering the Medicine Water. This is my dream, O Wise Ones! Tell me what it means.'

"They told him the striped lodge, painted red and black, meant that he would heal wounds, become a great Wise One among them. They said the picket pin showed that he would possess many horses, gifts from the men and women he had healed; and that the Otter and the White Bear would be his Helpers throughout his life on the world. They told him, too, that the Otter was his medicine, but said he would never become a chief, that he was too kindly to become even a great warrior. 'You are like the Person who led you beneath the Medicine Water,' they said. And this was all they told him.

"Next day the village moved, and when we passed the Medicine Water, we each dropped in a bead, or something else very pretty; so that the [dream] Father of The-fringe, and his Woman, might have them. This we have done ever since, when passing that way. And as long as there are Crow people they will continue to make such offerings to the Medicine Water, as they pass.

"All his life, just as the Wise Ones had said, The-fringe was a quiet, gentle man; and if he ever caused even the enemy any suffering, nobody ever heard about it. He joined many war-parties, but always returned without distinction, so that by our laws he could not marry until he was twenty-five. But besides his gentleness, The-fringe was bashful, and when he had reached thirty he was still single. People were smiling by this time; the women talking a little, of course.

"But every time a war-party left our village The-fringe went with it, and only one person in the whole tribe knew why he went. This person was a beautiful young woman, the daughter of one of our most successful warriors. She knew The-fringe loved her, that he hoped first to count coup and have his name spoken in council, so that he might pridefully ask her to marry him. She understood that he was too bashful to speak to her father until he had distinguished himself in some brave way, and there was nothing she could do about it but wait, since her lover would not avail himself of his right to marry, which his age now gave him.

"The year The-fringe was thirty we had a desperate fight with the Sioux, and in the battle a brother of this young woman was struck by an arrow that pierced his body below his arms. Its feathers stuck out of his armpit on the right side. He was going to his Father when they laid him down in the lodge.

"The-fringe was a powerful Wise One with many followers, by this time. He had many horses, and was popular, even though he was not a fighter. But no Wise One would ever *offer* to heal a sick or wounded man. It was necessary for somebody who was a relative of the suffering one to make request, if the services of a Wise One were needed. But when this young warrior was laid in his father's lodge, The-fringe saw his opportunity and told a close friend, 'I would try to heal that young man, if his people would ask me.'

"Of course they asked him. The young man's father came after The-fringe, himself. There was no time to waste. The-fringe at once stripped and began to paint his body.

" 'I will give you many horses, anything I possess, if you heal my son,' said the father, while The-fringe was painting himself.

" 'There is only one thing on the world I want,' answered The-fringe, looking across the lodge at the young woman he loved.

" 'I am willing,' she said. And that was the first anybody, besides themselves, knew they were in love. The young woman spoke out, because she was afraid The-fringe would not have the courage.

" 'It is well,' said her father, surprised. And while his helpers carried the wounded man to the chief's lodge by the river, The-fringe began to sing his Medicine Song.

"There was a sandy shore in front of the lodge, and the people formed a way from the lodge door to the water, in straight lines. But the helpers made the people near the water move back, so that the open way was shaped like the chief's lodge itself, its sharp point in the door.

"The-fringe wound a strip of otter skin around his head, tossed another strip, which had been cut so as to include the animal's tail, over his shoulder, and, singing to the drums of his helpers, lifted his medicine out of its bundle. It was a whole otter's skin, with the head stuffed. On the shoulders and cheeks of The-fringe I saw that there was mud, just as there always is on an otter's when he plays in the mud along a river. He whistled like an otter, dipped the medicine skin in a paunch kettle of water, and sprinkled it upon the wounded man, while the helpers sang to their drums.

"The young man sat up. Just then I could not see The-fringe, but I heard him whistle four times like an otter, and by and by beheld him coming out through the door of the lodge, followed by the wounded man.

"They walked into the river, where The-fringe dived like an otter, smoothly, and without disturbing the water. Four times he dived, twice upstream and twice downstream, while the otter skin seemed itself to be alive and swimming. Then I saw its nose at the wounds of the young man, saw its tail wiggle in the water as if it sucked blood and was pleased and its nose lift itself away from the wounds to let black blood fall on the water. But there was only a little of it. Red blood came quickly, and as quickly The-fringe stopped it. 'You are healed,' I heard him say. And this was true. The young man was well again. Two lumpy scars were where the holes had been."

Plenty-coups smoked awhile in silence, and when he spoke again, ended his story-telling. "I might tell you much more," he said, "but it would be nearly like the stories you already know. My life was much the same thing year after year, when I was young and strong. Now the old life is ended. Most of the men who knew it have gone, and I myself am eager to go and find them.

"All my life I have tried to learn as the Chickadee learns, by listening,—profiting by the mistakes of others, that I might help my people. I hear the white men say there will be no more war. But this cannot be true. There will be other wars. Men have not changed, and whenever they quarrel they will fight, as they have always done. We love our country because it is beautiful, because we were born here. Strangers will covet it and some day try to possess it, as surely as the sun will come tomorrow. Then there must be war, unless we have grown to be cowards without love in our hearts for our native land. And whenever war comes between this country and another, your people will find my people pointing their guns with yours. My heart sings with pride when I think of the fighting my people, the red men of all tribes, did in this last great war; and if ever the hands of my own people hold the rope that keeps this country's flag high in the air, it will never come down while an Absarokee warrior lives.

"Remember this, Sign-talker, and help my people keep their lands. Help them to hold forever the Pryor and Bighorn mountains. They love them as I do and deserve to have them for the help they have given the white man, who now owns all.

"I am old. I am not graceful. My bones are heavy, and my feet are large. But I know justice and have tried all my life to be just, even to those who have taken away our old life that was so good. My whole thought is of my people. I want them to be healthy, to become again the race they have been. I want them to learn all they can from the white man, because he is here to stay, and they must live with him forever. They must go to his schools. They must listen carefully to what he tells them there, if they would have an equal chance with him in making a living.

"I may be gone to my Father when you return here. I am very anxious to go where I may live again as men were intended to live. I am glad I have told you these things, Sign-talker. You have felt my heart, and I have felt yours. I know you will tell only what I have said, that your writing will be straight like your tongue, and I will sign your paper with my thumb, so that your people and mine will know I told you the things you have written down."

## AUTHOR'S NOTE

*Plenty-coups refused to speak of his life after the passing of the buffalo, so that his story seems to have been broken off, leaving many years unaccounted for. "I have not told you half that happened when I was young," he said, when urged to go on. "I can think back and tell you much more of war and horse stealing. But when the buffalo went away the hearts of my people fell to the ground, and they could not lift them up again. After this nothing happened. There was little singing anywhere. Besides," he added sorrowfully, "you know that part of my life as well as I do. You saw what happened to us when the buffalo went away."*

*I do know that part of his life's story, and that part of the lives of all the Indians of the Northwestern plains; and I did see what happened to these sturdy, warlike people when the last of the buffalo was finally slaughtered and left to decay on the plains by skin-hunting white men.*

*The Indian's food supply was now gone; so too were the materials for his clothes and sheltering home. Pitched so suddenly from plenty into poverty, the Indian lost his poise and could not believe the truth. He was dazed, and yet so deep was his faith in the unfailing bounty of his native land that even when its strange emptiness began to mock him he be-*

*lieved in the return of the buffalo to the plains, until white men began to settle there, their wire fences shutting off his ancestral water-holes. Then a bitterness tempered by his fatalism found a place in the Indian's heart, while a feeling of shame for the white man's wantonness was growing up in my own. The Indian was a meat eater, and now there was no meat. He had followed the buffalo herds up and down the land, or visited the foothills and mountains for elk, deer and bighorn, so that his camps had always been clean. Now, confined to reservations often under unsympathetic agents, his camps became foul, and he could not move them. Twice, in earlier days, white men had brought scourges of smallpox to the Indians of the Northwestern plains, and each time many thousands had died. Now, with the buffalo gone and freedom denied him, the Indian was visited by two equally hideous strangers, famine and tuberculosis. He could cope with neither. His pride was broken. He felt himself an outcast, a pariah, in his own country.*

*It was now that Plenty-coups, already a young war chief, became the real leader of his people. There were then among the Crows two older and more renowned warriors, but it was Plenty-coups who saw quite clearly that a readjustment of his people to meet the changing conditions was necessary. Gifted with the power of impressive speech, and possessing a dignity of presence that readily won him any hearing, he more than once visited the Indian Department at Washington in the interests of his people who were quick to recognize him as the outstanding Crow of his time. Giving advice to his people, he took care to follow it himself; he began early to cultivate the land, he established himself in a log house, and he even opened a general merchandise store where his tribesmen might trade, forever counseling his customers to be friendly with the white men whose encroachments were maddening to his people.*

*An official of the Burlington Railway Company who had dealings with Plenty-coups when purchasing a right of way through the Crow country for his road, recently wrote me: "I found him fair. He is wise and able; a real statesman"—a great compliment, coming as it did from a modern business man.*

*In spite of all that happened to prejudice him, Plenty-coups was always a patriotic American. When the United States declared war against Germany the aged chief of the Crows urged his young men to offer themselves as soldiers, often expressing the wish that he might, himself, go to the front and fight. So devoted was he, and so widely known in his advocacy of good feeling between his own people and white men, that he was chosen, as the representative of all the Indian tribes, to place the red man's wreath of flowers upon the grave of the Unknown Soldier at Arlington.*

*Because old-time redmen of the Northwest dated births by events in their tribal histories, or by extremely freakish seasons, there is often room for error in naming the year of an old Indian's nativity, according to our calendar. Plenty-coups may easily have been several years older than he believed. Any-*

*how, I know that he was weary, and that he was ready, even a little anxious, to go to "The Beyond-country" when the call came to him on the fourth of March, 1932. May he, my old friend, find the buffalo there, and live with them forever in perpetual summer.*

# INDEX

## A NOTE ABOUT THE AUTHOR

FRANK B. LINDERMAN (1869-1938) was born in Ohio and in 1885 went to Montana. His early years there were spent as trapper, hunter, and cowboy. For more than forty years he made his home in a cabin in the woods at Goose Bay on the shores of Flathead Lake, where he was intimately associated with the Crows and other Indian tribes of that section and was adopted by the Chippewas and Crees into their tribes. He was the author of *On a Passing Frontier, Lige Mounts, Free Trapper,* several books of Indian legends, and two books of verse.